OVERCOMING
THE
SUPERWOMAN
SYNDROME

To: Kenyetta
my dear friend, thank you for your support.
Stay Blessed!
Magfiling #5/9/07

D0932044

Edited by Linda Ellis Eastman

Professional Woman Publishing
Prospect, Kentucky

Published by:
Professional Woman Publishing
Post Office Box 333
Prospect, KY 40059
(502) 228-0906
http://www.prowoman.net

Please contact the publisher for quantity discounts.

ISBN 13: 978-0-9791153-6-3
ISBN 10: 0-9791153-6-1

Library of Congress Cataloging-In-Publication Data

Cover Design and Typography by:
Sential Design, LLC — www.sentialdesign.com

Printed in the United States of America

For my daughter and friend, Patty Eastman Lickliter,
for her loving compassion and care for others.

TABLE OF CONTENTS

TABLE OF CONTENTS
-CONTINUED-

TABLE OF CONTENTS
-CONTINUED-

ABOUT THE AUTHOR

LINDA EASTMAN

Linda Ellis Eastman is President and CEO of The Professional Woman Network (PWN), an International Training and Consulting Organization on Women's Issues. She has designed seminars which have been presented in China, the former Soviet Union, South Africa, the Phillipines, and attended by individuals in the United States from such firms as McDonalds, USA Today, Siemens-Westinghouse, the Pentagon, the Department of Defense, and the United States Department of Education.

An expert on women's issues, Ms. Eastman has certified and trained over one thousand women to start consulting/seminar businesses originating from such countries as Pakistan, the Ukraine, Antigua, Canada, Mexico, Zimbabwe, Nigeria, Bermuda, Jamaica, Costa Rica, England, South Africa, Malaysia, and Kenya. Founded in 1982 by Linda Ellis Eastman, The Professional Woman Network is committed to educating women on a global basis regarding, self-esteem, confidence building, stress management, and emotional, mental, spiritual and physical wellness.

Ms. Eastman has been featured in USA Today and listed in Who's Who of American Women, as well as Who's Who of International Leaders. In addition to women's issues, Ms. Eastman speaks internationally regarding the importance of human respect as it relates to race, color, culture, age, and gender. She will be facilitating an international conference where speakers and participants from many nations will be able to discuss issues that are unique to women on a global basis.

Linda Ellis Eastman is also founder of The Professional Woman Speakers Bureau and The Professional Woman Coaching Institute. Ms. Eastman has dedicated her businesses to increasing the self-esteem and personal dignity of women and youth around the world.

Contact
The Professional Woman Network
P.O. Box 333
Prospect, KY 40059
(502) 566-9900
lindaeastman@prodigy.net
www.prowoman.net
www.protrain.net

INTRODUCTION

Linda Ellis Eastman

With the fast pace of today's lifestyles, women so often are caught up in the "Be All Things to All People" Syndrome a.k.a. The Superwoman Syndrome. While running on the treadmill of life, you may have found yourself simply breathless and not feeling that you accomplished your tasks to the BEST of your abilities. For many of us the word GOOD is not in our vocabulary. We constantly strive to accomplish everything possible in a PERFECT manner.

We dedicate more time to other people and projects than to ourselves and eventually we must pay the price. The price tag for this constant stress is huge as it affects relationships, business, emotions, our bodies, and our minds.

The chapters in this book will "talk" to you, I am certain. The authors have written chapters that will set you on the right direction and path toward a better feeling of self while at the same time creating a less stressful life. This book will help you step off the treadmill and into a more healthy life emotionally, mentally, and physically.

Overcoming the Superwoman Syndrome is written for every woman who has ever looked into the mirror and asked herself "Why I am doing this to myself?" It is time now to take the journey to higher self-esteem that is predicated upon accepting yourself without having to be perfect.

Linda Ellis Eastman

OVERCOMING
THE
SUPERWOMAN
SYNDROME

ABOUT THE AUTHOR

LINDA ROSE MONGELL

Linda Rose Mongell is President and CEO of Marketing Me, a personal and professional consulting firm focused on enhancing image, brand and culture. She is an accomplished speaker, facilitator, trainer and consultant with more than 25 years in the corporate environment.

Linda Rose has extensive experience and a diverse background in the areas of marketing, executive management, strategic development, retail, public relations and communications, professional development, promotions, sponsorship management, event marketing, new business development, training, facilitation, process management and project and event production. She has also designed and developed needs assessments, communication and marketing strategies and various training programs and systems.

Linda Rose holds a B.A. in Public Relations and Communications and is a certified trainer in the areas of diversity, women's issues, brand and image building, as well as a certified coach from the Professional Woman Network. She is a member of the International Professional Woman Network (PWN), American Management Association (AMA), American Society for Training and Development (ASTD), and National Association for Female Executives (NAFE).

To add to her list of credentials, Linda Rose is a published author and is also a professional belly dancer and has taught belly dancing for beginners.

Contact
Marketing Me
717 ½ Poinsettia Avenue
Corona Del Mar, Ca 92625
E-mail: lrmongell@marketingme.com
Website: marketingme.com
Phone: 714.296.1472

ONE

OVERCOMING BEING ALL THINGS TO ALL PEOPLE

By Linda Rose Mongell

When you first hear "being all things to all people", what comes to mind? Gosh, I would love to be that person! Cool, must be superwoman. Let's dive a little deeper to discover its true meaning. Consider Amber, for example. She is invited to a concert that she has been looking forward to for months. She gets a panicked phone call from her sister that she needs Amber to come and baby sit, because she has been called in to work the graveyard shift at the hospital. In typical Amber fashion, she rushes to the aid of her sister. Imagine how upset Amber feels, and the disappointment that she gave up the concert. In another example, Tammy has taken a week of vacation over the holidays. She has a list of things she is planning to do, because she has been so busy that she allowed some things to slip. So she has planned out this week for herself to get caught up. She gets a call from her Mom about helping her alter a dress she wants to wear for New Year's Eve. Tammy has the expertise in that area, and like a good daughter, agrees to alter the dress. After a day of pulling all of the seams out of the dress, Tammy realizes the dress needs to be completely remade. She speaks to her Mom and her Mom starts in about really wanting to wear the dress on New Year's Eve, reminding her of how she should "help her mother". Tammy finishes the dress on New Year's Eve day, just in time for her Mom to tell her she changed her mind about going out that night. Imagine the anger and resentment Tammy felt after sacrificing her entire vacation to do what she thought was a good thing, only to feel taken advantage of by her own mother! Do you recognize these behaviors in yourself or someone you know? These behaviors are often called "Being All Things to All People." These behaviors may not look exactly the same in different individuals, but the outcomes are similar – individuals get upset, feel disappointment, anger and resentment (to name a few), and their lives are generally out of balance.

Maybe you can relate to the previous stories, or perhaps you have your own. Maybe you know someone who exhibits these "Being All Things to All People" behaviors on a regular basis. These behaviors may exist, but there is another real problem when you attempt to change your ways. People are not going to be happy with you saying "no". In this chapter you will look at what drives a person to be all things to all people, identify some of the consequences, and then review the methodology to overcome being all things to all, so that you achieve adequate balance in your life.

How would you define being all things to all people? Could it be that you are always helping people? Do you change the way you act or behave among people in order to be accepted? Are you always giving of yourself in some way to make someone else happy? Are you always trying to rescue someone and make them feel better? These behaviors most always start off with good intentions. However, after awhile you may begin to feel guilty or inadequate; to prove yourself and feel accepted, you resort to being all things to all people *all of the time.*

What drives you to that point where you are all things to all people? There are certainly personality traits that contribute, such as being kind-hearted, good natured, and nurturing. Of course, you can add to the list: being reliable, responsible, caring, giving, compassionate, empathetic, and sympathetic, to name a few. You become someone to lean on, that person who will always be there, that tower of strength. Maybe you have a difficult time saying "no." Maybe family and peer pressures get the best of you. Regardless of why you have become all things to all people, most often you don't know when to put on the brakes.

There is nothing wrong with helping your friends, family, co-workers, putting in extra hours at the office on occasion, volunteering and helping others solve the world's problems (unless, of course, it has meant compromising yourself!)

The cost can be far greater than you may ever realize, but you often don't come to that realization until it's too late. At some point in your doing good for everyone else (and being available to them at all times at your own expense), you may wake up one morning and wonder, "Whatever happened to me and my dreams? Who's going to be there for me when I need someone?" The greatest investment you can make is in yourself. If you aren't there for yourself, you can't be there for anyone else.

Have you considered your feelings and the affect it has on you when you give so much of yourself to others? Have you considered the risks involved by being all things to all people? Do you rationalize your behavior and say things like: "I am making them happy;" "I am doing things for everyone," "My days are filled with activities," or "I feel good about what I am doing." It's fine to feel good about being there for others, so long as you have balance in your life.

Let's consider some of those risks while you're so busy being all things to all people. Over time you may lose your sense of self. Who have you become? What have you sacrificed and given up? You forget who you are at your very core. What are you all about? What satisfies you? What are *your* needs? You risk losing what truly matters. Maybe it's losing someone very close to you who decides he or she can no longer watch you do *everything* for everyone else, and leaves. Or perhaps it's losing your sense of well being because you have given away all the time in your day, so you can't take care of your health with exercise, walking, or massage. What about your self-worth? Did you compromise the investment you needed to make so that you could be the best person you could be? (Maybe you sacrificed further education, starting your own business, or reading about topics of interest.) And what about those ill feelings you begin to carry around with you? Feelings such as anger, resentment, frustration and disappointment may have begun to surface. Have you become resentful, unfulfilled, and tired? You may have begun to feel that whatever you do is never enough. You may have reached a state where you forget that the more you tend to give others, *the more they will take.* Where are you in the picture? Are your needs being met? Do you truly feel good about yourself? What about the time you need for YOU? Is there any left?

You stop asking yourself, "What are my dreams and aspirations?" "What do I love to do?" "Where is my peace and serenity?" "Who am I really?" You begin to settle for someone else's life—their dreams, their hopes and aspirations, and meeting their needs. You must recognize that you can only fully give of yourself when you have a solid core from which to pull, and only when you have spent the time to develop yourself as the unique, wonderful, spiritual individual that you are. You can then give, volunteer, and be there for others *on your terms*. Reach a place where you are confident, so that no one and nothing can pull so much from you that you reach a place that you don't recognize, a place where you don't belong and don't know how to get out.

You have heard this before: "You are in charge of your own destiny." You are in charge of making the decisions for yourself. No one is going to come and rescue you. You need to rescue yourself! Every morning when you get up you have choices to make. What will you choose? You can continue doing for everyone else, or you can step up and be there for yourself first. If your decision is to step up, I will help you get there.

Once you have reached this place of being all things to all people, how do you stop these destructive behaviors? This is one area I can speak to from experience and with clarity. I was once one of these people. As an individual and a professional, I have developed and utilized a methodology – a set of steps and tools – that will lessen or eliminate destructive behaviors associated with this condition. (The worksheets are at the end of the chapter.) I must admit, it will not always be easy. Changing behaviors will require an every-day, every-moment focus. Not everyone will be supportive of the resulting changes. Those that have benefited from the past behaviors may begin to feel insecure and fearful that they are being abandoned. They will continue to "pull on your apron strings" and try every angle to keep the current behaviors because they are the beneficiaries. To attain these new desired behaviors for yourself does not mean running from responsibilities. The methodology I am sharing will help create boundaries, define an individual's core, and put time aside every day to nurture the spirit and the soul. Changes in long-engrained behaviors take time and patience. Give yourself permission to slip up now and then. But if we want change and are clear on what we want the outcomes to be, smarter choices can be made to eliminate the destructive behaviors that support Being All Things to All People.

Methodology Tips and Tools

Step 1: Recognize the Condition

The best way to begin to identify if you have become all things to all people is to ask yourself the following questions:

Question	Yes ✔	No ✔
Do I take time out of my day for me?		
Do I have personal goals, and if so, what have I accomplished lately for myself?		
Do I always put other people's needs ahead of my own?		
Am I always tired?		
Do I get frustrated easily?		
Is my schedule so full that I don't have time to think?		
Do I feel guilty when I say no?		

Am I afraid to say no?		
Do I feel obligated to always lend a helping hand?		
Do I measure my self-worth by doing for others?		
Have I adjusted my personality in anyway to be accepted by others?		
Am I afraid that if I am not there for someone, people will think I am inadequate?		
Do I place importance on what people think about me?		
Is being perfect important to me?		
Do I feel the need to be accepted by everyone around me?		
Do I feel pressured by my family, peers or society?		
Do I believe that if I put myself first, I will appear selfish?		
Have I sacrificed any of my aspirations?		

Step 2: Identify what you have lost sight of.

What have you risked? What have you sacrificed?

_____

_____

_____

Step 3: Identify Where You Want to Invest Your Energy

Ask yourself – am I the person I want to be? Describe that person. Is my life consistent with my aspirations and values? What are your aspirations? Where do you want to invest your time?

_____

_____

_____

Step 4: Allocate Time Every Day for You

Start with 15 minutes. You can spend time praying, reflecting, exercising, or journaling. Whatever you decide to do, make sure it is solely for you. Review your list of aspirations, if that will help you stay focused. Use this time wisely to reconnect with yourself. I would recommend time in the morning, so that you don't get caught up in the everyday activities, and then run out of time for you. Once you have managed to find fifteen minutes everyday, try to increase that gradually. I would recommend working up to one hour devoted to you.

Make a note of what time every day you are going to put aside for yourself. What will you be doing during that time?

_____

_____

_____

Step 5: Know Your Limits & Define Your Boundaries

Try and think back to your frustrating moments, or when you felt you couldn't continue. What was it that pushed you too far? Did you take on too much? Did you run out of time to get things done? Are you often tired? Do you compromise one thing for something else? Define your boundaries. (When I mention boundaries, where do you draw the line and say enough is enough?) How far can someone push you before they have stepped over the line? Do you work weekends? Do you accept phone calls after a certain time at night?

Make a list of your boundaries.

_____

_____

_____

Step 6: Learn to Say No

This may be one of the most difficult tasks of all. Give yourself permission to say "no." You don't need to give people reasons or make excuses. Just say no. You may consider saying "no" on the phone rather than in person, if it is easier. I would prepare by reviewing your list of aspirations, or review the reasons and importance for saying "no" to give you more support. Always be prepared. Don't allow yourself to be caught off-guard. Being caught off-guard is one of the weakest times to be able to say "no" if this is a difficult task for you. The first couple of times may be rough, but trust me. It gets easier! (The sooner you do this rather than wavering, the easier it will become). Remember, this is what is right for you. You are honoring yourself.

Make a list of those people and things you need to say "No" to, and how you may go about it.

_____

_____

_____

Step 7: Empower the People Around You

Rather than doing and being all things to all people, teach them to do it themselves. Enable them, and give them the tools to be able to do what they need to do. Show them once, and then let them figure it out the next time. Help them find alternatives, and then step away. If you step back in and help, you are sending the message that you aren't serious and they can call on you again. You will need to start all over again, but mean it next time! You need to send the message that you aren't there anymore to do it for them.

List some of the steps you can take to empower the people around you.

_____

_____

_____

Step 8: Let Go of Needy Friends

We all have friends that drain us of our energy. These people are considered emotional vampires. They make any conversation or interaction with you all about them. Try to phase these people out of your life. If you can't, then spend very little time with them, so they can't drain you so much. Consider redirecting your energies away from them. Find other areas of focus. If you are able, redirect any conversations to happy, more positive discussions. Don't get sucked in. Again, this is where I would prepare for these encounters. Keep your focus and anticipate the interaction. Don't allow yourself to get caught off-guard. After a few encounters, they will realize you won't jump on their bandwagon, and they will back off.

Make a list of those needy friends you need to release. Make note of how you are going to do that.

_____

_____

_____

Step 9: Stop Succumbing to Family and Peer Pressures

This will take into account setting boundaries and learning to say no. I strongly recommend that you think through the encounters you have with family and friends as to where you get sucked into doing and being all things. You need to plan and prepare ahead of time, and arm yourself with your boundaries and the word "no" prior to connecting with them. If you are on the phone, write down your responses and keep them handy. If you are in person, rehearse your responses ahead of time.

List some action steps you want to take to address these pressures.

_____

_____

_____

Step 10: Celebrate Balance

Treat yourself to something wonderful when you have managed to create some balance in your life.

Make a list of a reward or incentive to begin to overcome being all things to all people.

_____

_____

_____

ABOUT THE AUTHOR

JAYNE M. FOUNTAIN, M.ED.

Jayne M. Fountain is the founder and CEO of The Fountain Institute for Professional Excellence and Director of Public Relations and Tourism for a private company. As a certified, professional speaker, trainer and coach, Ms. Fountain's presentations have been referred to as "dynamic", "highly motivational" and "life changing". With over twenty five years in education, private business and consulting, Ms. Fountain has worked with U.S. Department of State programs and presented in China, the former Soviet Union, Australia, New Zealand and throughout Europe. She has certifications in Professional Development, Diversity and Multi Culturalism, Women's Issues, and is an international consultant for Birkman International.

Ms. Fountain has been featured on Stop Gap Radio, The Travel Channel, and The Disney Channel and in Family Fun Magazine. She is the author of "The Amish Kitchen", "Grant Writing Made Easy" and is contributing author of "The Christian Woman's Guide to Personal Success". She is a regular presenter and keynote speaker specializing the "Overcoming Obstacles to Personal Success" and "Living a Life of Purpose, Passion and Power!" Based upon her own life, Ms. Fountain developed and presents "Recovery of the Broken Woman". In addition, she developed the WEL PROGRAM (Women's Empowerment Luncheons) and the INFO-NAR...Power in an Hour, one hour motivational and high impact presentations. In addition, she has facilitated the Summit on Citizen Diplomacy, developed the Transition into American Culture in Washington, D.C. and works with international visitors as a cultural liaison with the U.S. Department of State.

Ms. Fountain is totally dedicated to encouraging others to over come obstacles and to living a life of purpose and fulfillment. She guides others to restoration and purpose through her training and speaking and her one -on- one assessments and coaching.

Ms. Fountain serves on the International Board of Advisors to the Professional Woman Network, and is a member of the National Association of Female Executives, La Red Business Network, The National Council for International Visitors and Akron International Friendship.

Contact
The Fountain Institute for Professional Excellence
P.O. 170
Berlin, Ohio 44610
Phone: (330)473-0965
Website: www.fountaininstitute.com
Email: Jayne@fountaininstitute.com

TWO

THE ART OF THANKFULNESS

by Jayne Fountain

I'm guessing that you are reading this book because you know someone who has the Superwoman Syndrome. And maybe that person is YOU! For most of us, it began during childhood; we were driven to make good grades, to win 4-H competitions or spelling bees! And then in high school, we continued to strive to make good grades, but then we needed to look good, to be "acceptable" to our peers, to be the president of the clubs we belonged to, or the captain of the cheerleading squad, or all of the above!!! That cycle continued through college with more drive to achieve and then, many of us married and once again felt that we had to do all and be all.

We became so busy solving every problem in our office, taking care of our children and families, and making our homes beautiful, that along the way we began to forget some of the wonderful things that make life so satisfying. And as life would have it, in my case, my life came to an abrupt halt, and I began to see what I had given up along the way.

As a little girl from Georgia, I was raised in the church. And one of the scriptures that I learned was one that became a life lesson for me in overcoming my Superwoman Syndrome.

"Always to joyful. Keep on praying.
No matter what happens, always be thankful."
— I Thessalonians 5:18 NLT

Let me take you back to my experience a few years ago. As I walked to my kitchen window on a beautiful, hot day in July, sipping my freshly brewed cup of coffee, I saw at least ten neighbors in my perennial gardens pulling six-foot thistles, blankets of weeds, and piles of grass. As I viewed the sweat flowing off their brow, my heart was filled with a rush of gratitude. Even though kindness is a core element in my Ohio Amish community, being the recipient of their kindness and generosity, on such a hot and humid day, overwhelmed me.

Following a "cardiac event" some weeks earlier, I was unable to do the work in my gardens that in years past had brought me great joy. That joy had turned to stress as I watched the weeds overtake my beautiful flowers. I couldn't even do the simplest task of pulling weeds or planting perennials in my gardens. While watching my neighbors perform a task that poor health prevented me from doing, a sense of gratefulness overflowed in my heart. I was always the neighbor who had the beautiful perennial gardens. I was the neighbor who made sure that my gardens and house were magazine, picture perfect. But, now my life as I had known it had come to an abrupt halt. As I looked out my window and saw my wonderful, caring neighbors taking care of my gardens, my eyes filled with tears and my heart filled with gratitude.

For you see, the art of thankfulness is a HEART issue. We're taught to say "thank you" as a polite response and know that we should always thank others. But, as I watched my neighbors toil in the hot sun, I realized that thankfulness is so much more. It is the attitude that is truly reflected in the deepest part of our heart. And, when we are in the middle of high achievement and the "I have to do it all" attitude, that true sense of thankfulness is many times forgotten due to the demands of the day planner, the list of goals we have, and the tasks we want to accomplish. True thankfulness reflects a characteristic that is registered in the heart.... an attitude that is at times an unconscious state of being. But, on many occasions, it takes great effort to achieve a sense of thankfulness due to misfortune, ill health, grief or other disturbing circumstances.

The scripture that I learned as a child says, "In everything, give thanks." It is always easy to be thankful when things are going well in our lives. In fact, we generally become so comfortable during times of well being that we either forget to express true thankfulness, or just find time to murmur quick thanks.

But, sometimes our lives don't always go as we have planned. Life is full of unexpected ups and downs, disappointments and sadness. Sometimes these are situations that we have created for ourselves by making poor choices. But, many times, totally out of our control, tragedy, disappointments and unfulfilled dreams are part of our lives. These times bring us to our knees, either literally or figuratively. I believe that we are to give thanks in all things and at all times... when life is very good to us, and always when we feel crippled by the pain and disappointment.

On this particular day, I had no problem expressing my gratitude to my neighbors for their unselfish hours of toil. But, as with many of you, over my lifetime, there have been too many times to count when my heart was broken, or when I experienced great disappointments. I did not feel that amazing sense of gratefulness during those times like I had in my heart on that hot July day. During those times, it was difficult for me to even consider saying thank you to God or anybody else while in the midst of the pain I was feeling. But, during those times, I did cry out to God, and I was determined to become a more caring, empathetic individual, and one who was less judgmental about the situations that others found themselves in.

One of my greatest disappointments in life was the end of my twenty-five year marriage. I fought, I prayed, and I cried out to God to save my marriage and family, as I knew it. It had been a long, hard, abusive and demoralizing marriage, but I held onto the dream of what could be. I held onto the hope that I would not suffer the ultimate demise of my dreams. But, as with many of you, I experienced the painful realization that, no matter how much I loved, no matter now much I hoped and prayed, no matter how perfect I tried to make my home or take care of my family, I could not control the heart or the actions of another.

Over the years since, I have grieved the loss of my dreams and longings for that marriage, but my faith that all things can and do work together to make me a more caring individual, as well as a more successful woman of business, and pushed me forward. And, I began to practice being thankful, even though my heart was broken. It was so difficult to be thankful during a time when my heart was shattered as I left my twenty five year marriage of constant abuse and adultery with very little, while my former husband would live financially well and secure the rest of his life. But, I discovered an AMAZING RESULT of making the effort to look at all the things I had to be thankful for, even when I was in the middle of great sorrow. I began to experience joy. And now, I do rejoice that I live in an abuse-free environment. By determining that I would practice being thankful, I saw my life turn in a new direction, and I embarked on a new path that is greater than anything I could have imagined for me during that painful time. In the years since the end of my marriage, I have moved into living a full and joyful life. Today, my life overflows with thanksgiving for every day that I live, for every breath that I take, and for every person that I am privileged to meet. I did not feel any joy at the end of my marriage. However, applying the art of thankfulness has sustained me through that and other challenging times.

I encourage you to take a few minutes to recall a time that might have been truly hard for you. Think about how, during that time, you were able to experience a deep abiding joy that came from the thankfulness of the other many blessings in your life. I recall listening to the news recently following an especially bad storm that destroyed homes and property. As the interviewer was questioning an older couple who had lost their home, they looked at each other with tears in their eyes, and remarked that even though all of their worldly possessions were gone, they were thankful to have each other. Their joy was clearly reflected in their words during this time of loss and pain in their lives.

1. Do you recall a particularly painful time in your life?

2. What do you have in your life that you can practice being thankful for even during difficult times?

As a result of being an emotionally broken woman during a good portion of my marriage, at times I made some truly poor choices, reactive decisions and life changing mistakes that placed a great burden of pain into my children's lives. I recall vividly, following a traumatic event, when I felt particularly lost, unloved and disappointed in myself, that my three children enveloped me in their arms as I cried. The flood of gratefulness that I felt then, and the memory it brings to me now, can hardly be measured in words. I have been given the greatest gift of three, truly amazing human beings that I am honored to call my children. The thankfulness in my heart for them and their loving support and acceptance has sustained me through many very difficult times. My children have shown me constant love, acceptance and support during the times in my life when I could have made better decisions. My thankfulness for my children gave me something that I desperately needed during those hard times. I discovered that thankfulness develops STRENGTH within us. There have been times that I felt I simply could not go forward, but I became empowered by focusing on, and being thankful for, these three amazing people.

1.   Name three things in your life that you are truly thankful for.

2.   Name the ways that this attitude of thanksgiving empowers you.

Several years following my divorce, I knew it was time to make changes in my life, and to take the time to evaluate my purpose here on this Earth. It was during this time that I had an eye-opening encounter with an individual that shook me to the core of my being. This individual's honesty and kindness became the impetus for a forty-day intensive time of prayer and meditation for me. It was physically and emotionally exhausting, but it was a life changing experience for me.

Tears flowed from my eyes and my heart shattered as I realized that I had hidden the wonderful, loving and kind person that I was on the inside behind a mask of Type A, high performance, high achieving, and highly controlling behaviors. It protected me from the inadequacy and pain that I felt from abuse that had taken place in my life as a child, and the pain I had felt from my former husband's lack of love, attention and affection for me. I had been unfaithful to myself, just as my former husband had been unfaithful to me in our marriage. After hours of crying, exhausted and empty, I thanked God for who I was. I acknowledged honestly my faults, my abilities and my talents, and I expressed thankfulness for all of it! I determined then to learn to love myself, and to live a life that reflected who I really was and who I wanted to be. I had been a woman in so much pain, but with so much pride, that I would not allow anyone to see it. I reacted to pain in my life over and over by making poor choices or reactive choices that showed that I did not like or love myself. I determined to live an authentic life, a life that reflected purpose and passion, but was not a performance for someone else in an effort to try to gain or earn their love, praise or acceptance. I finally understood that the emptiness that I had tried to fill in my marriage, my career, and with my children, would not be filled until I accepted and loved myself for who I was. True thankfulness brings CLARITY to our minds.

1. Have you experienced an event in your life that changed your thinking or direction?

2. Name your faults, abilities and talents. Are you thankful for them all?

3. How does it make you feel to be thankful for your faults, as well as your abilities and talents?

Regardless of the circumstances in my life, I discovered that learning to be thankful for who I am and what I have, creates an environment of harmony. I believe that this is truly the greatest benefit of practicing the art of thankfulness. It is as though we are at war with ourselves, and we as women often beat ourselves up because we are not prettier, thinner, taller, shorter, or smarter than we are. It is imperative that you practice the art of thankfulness with yourself and for yourself. I discovered that peace can be ours even in the midst of conflict, extremely busy lives, and exhausting careers, when we practice thankfulness for who we are and all the attributes that make us the amazing women that we are! True thankfulness brings PEACE into our minds, spirit and lives.

1. Do you experience an inner sense of peace in your life?

2. If not, write down each of your attributes and verbally say aloud that you are thankful for each and every one.

The greatest reason for practicing and developing the art of thanksgiving is to discover who you are, and gain the power and integrity to live an honest and authentic life...one that is not lived to present an image of what we think others want to see or what we think is the "right" image to project. So many women are caught up in living that life.

For you see, the art of thankfulness REVEALS WHO WE REALLY ARE ON THE INSIDE. It is indeed a heart issue!! It is easy to say "thank you", to use words that are flattering, creative and beautiful, that are meant to portray to others that you are truly thankful. But, in the end, your actions will reflect the true nature of your heart. If you are truly grateful for the good and the bad, the happy and painful times, you will be as an open book. Others will be able to "read" the truth in you by observing your actions. We have all made mistakes, and we as human beings will make mistakes in the future. But, when a person is transparent and honest, there is an attitude of thankfulness that is evident in all that we do.

1. Do your actions indicate that you are a thankful person?

2. Do you need to change the way you treat others in order to exhibit the art of thankfulness?

One cannot write about the art of thankfulness without it bringing to mind individuals who have been walking examples of kindness, generosity, and concern for others. These people have made our lives richer, and encourage us to operate our lives with the principles of character. It is without reserve that I thank God for loving me enough to bring support, strength and unfailing love into my life through such individuals.

I am a woman of faith…not a perfect woman. I, too, have times when I wish I were taller, thinner, prettier, smarter, but because of my faith, I believe the following:

The Art of Thankfulness involves: (1) **Trusting God** to know what is best for you. He knows when your heart is broken. He knows when you are grieving. He lovingly holds your hand through the suffering, the loneliness and the sadness. The Art of Thankfulness involves (2) **A commitment to obey** principles of character and a commitment to give thanks in everything, in spite of feelings of pain, loss or emptiness. Once you make that commitment, it becomes easier to practice thanksgiving in the midst of confusion.

The Art of Thankfulness also involves (3) **Being a good steward** of all that you are and all that you have. We're all blessed with gifts such as children, comfortable homes, a loving family, and the gift of friendship with people who truly care about us and who are always there for us. Make a point to spend quality time on a regular basis with those people in your life.

Next, The Art of Thankfulness involves (4) **Coming to the end of yourself** and recognizing that the world does not revolve around your problems, your crises, or your needs. Your life takes on a new meaning and new value when you practice the art of thankfulness on a daily basis.

The Art of Thankfulness involves (5) **Making right** any wrong that you have done to others. For many of us who feel that we have made so many mistakes that it is impossible to even remember them all, just sit down and begin listing people that you know you have not been fair to. Perhaps, you would never think about literally stealing the inheritance of another, as some relatives have done. Or cheating a spouse out of shared assets. But you know that you have mistreated someone in some way. It may be that you were simply impatient with someone or unkind. Look for the opportunity to either undo what you have done, or ask the person you have wronged to forgive you.

Last, The Art of Thankfulness involves (6) **Evaluating your true attitude** and making sure that your intentions are pure and your heart is good and genuine. I spent a good portion of my life trying to be perceived as someone different than who I really was. As a result, God allowed me to make mistakes and to live the consequences of those mistakes. Recently, following a speech I had given to a women's international conference, a participant came up to me with tears flowing and said, "You touched the core of my being. You are so 'real'." God has changed me from a person trying to live an "image" of the perfect woman, wife, and mother, to an authentic person who is simply a woman who has made many mistakes, has been forgiven by her family and her friends, who is simply who she is: a flawed human being who is very thankful for all of those difficult times, all of my flaws and talents, and for the very special friends and family that I have.

Practicing true thankfulness will bring you joy, strength, clarity and peace even during those challenging times in your life. I encourage you to make a commitment today to walk through your life with a sense of gratefulness and thanksgiving. You will experience the incredible fullness in your spirit and life. Make the commitment to be thankful in a way that displays a grateful spirit, honorable behavior, and sense of joy. Determine now to practice The Art of Thankfulness.

Questions:

1. How can I remind myself today that I have much to be thankful for?

2. What would my friends and family say that I am most grateful for? What do I want it to be?

3. What has happened to me that once was considered painful, but now has reshaped my life for the better?

4. How should I change the way I live today in order to reflect a greater sense of thankfulness?

This chapter is dedicated to those who have taught me the art of thankfulness: Marianne Stutzman, Granny Mary and Papa Cecil, Rich Andrade, Miguel Cantos, Saylor, and from the very moment they entered this world, my precious children: Misty, Rhett and Matt.

ABOUT THE AUTHOR

DAWN HARRIS

Ms. Harris is President and CEO of The Harris Institute for Professional Excellence. She received her MBA from Woodbury University in Burbank, California and her undergraduate degree in Biochemistry at the Cal Poly State University in San Luis Obispo, California. Ms. Harris has worked in the Medical Device industry as a Manager of Regulatory Training. Prior to this capacity, she worked in the biotechnology industry for over nine years in a variety of departments such as Quality Assurance, Manufacturing, Internal Audit, and Corporate Finance.

As a Certified Customer Service Trainer, Dawn Harris is committed to teaching individuals the importance of a professional image, positive attitude development, and business etiquette. As a Certified Diversity Trainer, she is passionate about training companies and individuals regarding the importance of exclusivity vs. inclusivity, and building teams among diverse corporate cultures. Ms. Harris has co-authored *Customer Service & Professionalism for Women* and *The Young Woman's Guide for Personal Success*.

Contact:
The Harris Institute for Professional Excellence
(443) 266-4066
dharris@theharrisinstitute.com
www.protrain.net

THREE

OFF THE WALL! DEALING WITH ANGER

By Dawn M. Harris

I was locked in a one-way conversation with a demon. My heart pounded with anger as we stood there, nose to nose. She hissed venomous words through clinched teeth, so close to me I could smell her dinner. Her fury rang in my ears like a hammer striking hot iron. *Stop!* I yelled at her in my mind. *Just be quiet and go away!*

But the tirade continued as she bellowed out words that cut me with surgical precision. I wanted to curse back at her, to counter her thrusts with equal vigor and venom. The anger rushed through my veins like a roaring fire. The torture went on until my senses began to grow numb. The demon's voice grew dim as I thought about other things I had to do: *I've got to get my laundry done today, and then the car. I must wash the car! Is it time for an oil change? I have so much to do.*

Now, totally numbed by the demon's endless vindictive rampage, my eyes had glossed over.

Then, I heard the word that caused this story to be written, "BITCH". Whip-lashed back to my reality, I backed away in horror and turned my back to the demon. *Not you,* I thought to myself. *Of all people, not you!* After all of these years, trying to be "the best" at everything I was asked to do, I was reduced to a five-letter word.

Suddenly my senses sharpened. Everything moved in slow motion as I spun around, as if suspended in thin air. It was like a scene from the movie *Matrix.* I took two giant steps forward with a clinched fist, prepared to throw her out of my room. Well…that was the plan anyway. Thank God my oldest sister came, seemingly out of nowhere, and intercepted me before I could land the punch. My sister, now Ring Master, separated us, and at that very moment I began to feel the momentum of the unreleased anger magnify inside me. I was filled with disappointment in myself, and heartbroken because of the negatively espoused views that were spewed at me. I focused my anger on the closet door of my room and kicked it with everything I had. I pulled my leg out of the hole I created, not feeling the jagged edges cutting into my shin and calf. The cuts were so deep that my muscle tissue was exposed. Within seconds a gush of blood appeared.

My leg healed long before my heart. The event was a turning point in my life; a recognition of my own rage and limits to which I could be pushed. I stayed mad and hurt for days, not wanting to resolve anything. Needless to say, things did not stay that way for too long. My mother was the bigger person, and she began the dialogue that healed the emotional wounds of our shameful disagreement. However, the teenage girl I once was, no longer existed. That childhood innocence was lost forever.

I view this turning point in my life as a gateway to helping me understand my anger, which became a key to one of many personal freedoms. However, with freedom comes responsibility. Therefore, expressing anger wisely is prudent, not only because it is healthy, but also because of its potentially destructive and volatile nature.

It is my hope that this chapter will equip you with tools to help you deal with anger at home and in the workplace.

I use myself as an example because in my view, theory and practice are two different types of teachers. After the aforementioned incident, I promised myself that I would never allow myself to become out of control again, and sat and reflected on ways to begin to take control of my anger. During this process, I identified four ways.

I began with *acknowledging my range of anger*. Secondly, I *explored how I typically express anger*. The third area I focused on was defining *the source of my anger*. Lastly, *I sought forgiveness*, which was the hardest to achieve.

Being angered, enraged, and losing all ways of rational thinking is interesting to me. You never really know the depths of these feelings until you are pushed. Although you may have an idea of how far you could go, you may still surprise yourself. Take a mixture of a bad day at the office, traffic, a failed relationship, and poor school grades all happening simultaneously, and see how you react! Pressure and stress have a way of manifesting themselves in peculiar ways. Without being tested, you really never know what you are made of. Therefore, I believe in putting preventive measures in place to lessen the blows that life may bring.

In the space provided below, describe a time when you were "pushed to your limit" and expressed anger in a way that surprised you.

_____

_____

_____

_____

I believe there are two types of expressions for anger 1) In-the-moment anger and 2) Post-traumatic stress. I define "In-the-moment anger" as the visceral emotional anger you feel at the time you are experiencing it. This is the type of anger that makes some people quietly stand up, go to their top drawer, and get a gun or shout at the top of their lungs.

"Post-traumatic-stress" is the silent reflection experienced when the argument has ended and you are by yourself thinking about who angered you and why. It is the time when you are able to be honest with yourself (if you choose) to recount the good, bad, ugly, right and wrong elements of the situation that angered you.

One key to releasing anger is discovering the source of it. Whether the source is a failed relationship, your family or job, identifying it will allow you to deal with anger more quickly. Sometimes it is the little things that may "set us off", but the source of our anger is totally unrelated. When you find yourself overreacting, feeling on edge, or yelling at the car in front of you, the anger that you may be feeling could be misplaced. It could be coming from a myriad of places that are out of sync in your life. This concept of eliminating anger by identifying your anger style is supported by Ron Potter-Efron, M.S.W., author of _Letting Go of Anger_.

Potter-Efron identifies triggers that can make a person launch down the path to anger in an instant. One example he uses is performance reviews. Let's say your manager or supervisor gives you feedback that you are slow at getting your work completed. Avoid becoming the "Cornered Dog", as Potter-Efron terms. If you feel you have just been attacked, you may be feeling "shameful anger", and you may want to lash out. Potter-Efron suggests that this reaction may become leverage for others to conclude that you are insecure, which makes you look weak and may further validate the criticism. Instead of traveling down the alluring path of anger and seeking revenge, first try slowing down your reaction.

If the assessment is accurate, try focusing on ways to improve it. If the feedback is not accurate, before lashing out, Potter-Efron suggests that the best way to respond to an unwarranted criticism is to let the pain fade and "deliver a calm and well-considered reproach". In my opinion, it is a far more rational way in which to respond to disappointment or unmet expectations in the workplace.

The second workplace example Potter-Efron offers is dealing with "incompetent coworkers". Although he uses this example primarily for men who shun the urge to rage, this anger is often expressed in other ways, and shared by men and women alike. They include anxiety, fatigue, or destructive behavior (such as cheating or drinking). So, as to avoid becoming "The Redirector", Potter-Efron suggests talking out frustration even when you cannot see what good can come from it. Start by initiating dialogue with the person that upset you by saying something respectful to the person first, then begin to explain what bothered you. This can create a plan to avoid a repeat occurrence in the future.

In my view, anger is not a bad emotion. It serves a purpose. I believe it is what we do with this emotion and how it is released that determines the outcome.

In the spaces provided below, list the triggers of your anger. Next to each trigger, write why the particular incident or feedback upset you.

_____

_____

_____

_____

If you could relive the incidents when the above triggers were experienced, what would you have done differently?

_____

_____

_____

_____

My belief is that identifying the source of your anger is critical to its release and is also shared by Howard Richman of Sound Feelings Publishing. He suggests several healthy ways of releasing stress. One way is to "give yourself permission to express anger". He states, "It is not wrong to express anger, fear, sadness, or rage. In fact, it is healthy to release these emotions regularly. What is wrong is when we hurt someone in the process."

Another way he suggests to reduce the anger-stress is by combining mental and physical effort. "Mental therapy alone may be extremely helpful for anger release, but it can only take you so far. Similarly, the physical act of doing exercise can help many people let off steam, but it may not remove deep-seated anger. The most effective process is when you can combine both the mental and physical effort. This is when you do a particular physical activity along with the mental intention of releasing the anger."

Additionally, he suggests that totally letting go of your emotions is also important. In a safe environment you can express yourself by shouting (if you can find a secluded area at work or even the inside of your car) may afford instant relief.

In my view, the hardest and most painful part of the journey is dealing with anger once it has been expressed and learning forgiveness. In my view, forgiveness and damage are proportional. For instance, if the damage was irreparable (physically hitting my Mother), then my road to repairing my relationship with my mother, watching her heal and becoming "okay" with myself, would have taken years for me. I might be angry with myself for years, if I did not apologize for my anger toward her, learn from my mistake, and forgive myself.

I believe forgiveness is not for the other person. It is for ourselves! It is a process of taking back the control of a wasted emotion and putting focus and loving energy back on us. We become the victor when we do not allow the situation or person to keep us unsettled and emotional about an issue or incident that is in the past.

In the spaces provided below, list events or situations for which you eventually forgave yourself and/or another person. What did you do and how long did it take for you to totally forgive them or yourself?

_____

_____

_____

_____

List the people you feel you need to forgive in the next few months and why you have not forgiven them, yet. Do they know that you are still upset with them?

_____

_____

_____

_____

Without warning, anger can well up within us and before we know it, we have lashed out at someone or something. Although anger cannot always be avoided (either at home or in the workplace), we have to find healthier ways of dealing with anger. With demanding social and work schedules, family and friends can push us to a "boiling point"! But by knowing our range of anger, our proclivity to it, and ways to release it, we can get closer to forgiving ourselves and others, and to leading a happier and healthier life.

In the spaces provided below, list some ways that you are going to apply your behavior to understand your range of anger. How you will release it and forgive yourself and others?

_____

_____

_____

_____

Notes:

_____

_____

_____

_____

_____

_____

_____

_____

_____

_____

_____

_____

_____

_____

_____

_____

_____

_____

_____

_____

_____

_____

ABOUT THE AUTHOR

ROSEMARY BONILLA

Rosemary Bonilla currently resides in Staten Island, New York with her husband and two children aged twenty and thirteen. She has over twenty years experience in the healthcare industry with ten years at a management level and is currently pursuing a Master's Degree in Health Administration. She has taught Medical Billing/Coding at Wagner College in Staten Island, New York. Ms. Bonilla is president and CEO of the profitable medical billing company, president and CEO of a real estate holding company, as well as a practice manager for the Department of Radiology at Maimonides Medical Center.

She holds memberships with the New York State Real Estate Association, National Association of Female Executives, Radiology Business Management Association, Medical Group Management Association, New Day Toastmasters, Fellow in the American College of Medical Practice Executives, and is an International Advisory Board member of The Professional Woman Network.

Rosemary Bonilla is a Certified Trainer in personal and professional development and conducts seminars and workshops nationally and internationally specializing in developing a positive self-image, financial freedom and personal and professional development. She is also available for personal and professional coaching sessions.

Contact:
Rosemary Bonilla
Faculty Practice Manager
Radiology Department
Maimonides Medical Center
4802 Tenth Avenue
Brooklyn, NY 11219
(718) 283-6157
rbonilla@maimonidesmed.org
www.protrain.net

FOUR

SELF–SABOTAGE: OVERCOMING SELF–DEFEATING HABITS

By Rosemary Bonilla

What is self-sabotage? It is the opposite of self-care! Let us define both words in order to truly understand them.

- Self – sabotage = to damage one's own nature or personality

- Self – care = to think that one's own nature or personality is important and/or interesting

Self-sabotage is when it seems that you have everything going for you, and you engage in some sort of self-defeating behavior that either hurts you or your goals and dreams. You know what you are supposed to do, but don't do it. You have a hidden, greater need on the inside that is holding you back.

Your mind set is not prosperous if it is filled with limitations and personally imposed barriers. It should be filled with prosperity and limitless possibilities. You have to expand your mind and **believe yourself to be of value, in order for anything of value to come into your life**. Self-care shows you are an important and interesting valuable human being. You are worthy to receive all that this world has to offer. Your potential is limitless. You can achieve your dreams and attain the desires of your heart. You are saying, "I deserve to take care of myself."

If you cannot love yourself, how can you love another? You are a unique individual, with talents and gifts to give to this world and to yourself. You can begin to build a new, improved self-image today! It is not the image that someone else told you that you *should be*, but the image *you can be* with the proper positive self-affirmations. Imagine having control of your time, your money, your weight and your career!

Self-Sabotage Habits

One of the most common habits of self-sabotage is **procrastination**. This habit is a killer to many dreams and goals! If your vocabulary is full of "can't" and "should", then be prepared to do the exercises in this chapter. They will help you with overcoming such bad habits as procrastination, or simply, putting off things which should be done NOW! Take a look at this list and consider whether you are guilty of any of these habits:

Self-Sabotage Habits:	
1. Procrastination	
2. Overindulgence In Eating, Drinking, or Spending	
3. Act Impulsively/Don't Think About the Consequences	
4. Get Distracted or Lose Focus on Goals or Dreams	
5. Skip Exercising	
6. Eat Poorly	
7. Take on Too Many Projects	
8. Ignore or Minimize Problems in Relationships, Job or Health	
9. Hold Unrealistic Expectations	
10. Too Critical or Judgmental of Yourself or Others	
11. Need Help But Do Not Ask For It	
12. Rush Through Projects	
13. Obsess Over a Trip, Purchase or Other Decision	
14. Overestimate the Risks of Something Bad Happening	
15. Worry Too Much	
16. Impulse buy	

List ways in your personal life you have sabotaged your own personal success.

Example: You constantly overspend and over-charge on your credit card. You are "maxed" and it impacting your credit. You feel that you are a "shopaholic", and yet constantly buy more shoes, cosmetics, and jewelry than you need.

1. _____

2. _____

3. _____

What strategies can you use to be sure that you don't sabotage yourself again in these areas?

Example: You leave your credit card at home (or give it to your husband or significant other for safe-keeping). By not having your credit card with you when you feel the impulse to buy, you will find that you will not be able to continue your impulse buying. You will have set self-boundaries in place.

1. _____

2. _____

Learn to be good to yourself and to allow yourself to have personal successes. Many women practice self-sabotage rather than self-care, because they do not feel that they deserve success! (Do you deserve to have money in the bank, accept promotions at work, lose weight, exercise, or feel good about yourself?) But self-exploration takes time and lots of self-evaluation. Sometimes we need to seek therapy, counseling, take immediate action, visualize and use imagery of our potential success, journal, listen to tapes, read books, pray, or meditate to find the answers. Whatever it takes, you need to remind yourself that you are deserving of good things, and you don't deserve to undermine all the wonderful goals and dreams you have for yourself.

Another way we may practice self-sabotage is by blaming others. Rather than being responsible for our own actions, we may constantly blame others for our poor feelings of self. Stop the blame game! The best way to empower yourself is to feel like a survivor rather than a victim! Learn to take care of yourself by **parenting yourself.** Perhaps you have been told by others during your childhood that you were really no good, stupid, overweight, or simply not wanted. You felt that you didn't deserve anything of worth. Rather than hold onto these feelings and allow the past to control your behaviors now, learn to let go of the anger and resentment. We can learn to parent the child within. Oftentimes, it is really that hurting child within each of us that may be at the root of why we constantly undermine our own success by self-sabotage. Remember, you are worthy of success and happiness. Allow these things, which are good, to come into your life.

What are your goals and dreams? Name your top three and write them down

1. _____
2. _____
3. _____

Write down a listing of unhealthy habits (self-defeating behaviors) you have exhibited, and healthy ones that you can build into your life now:

Unhealthy Habits	Healthy Habits
1.	1.
2.	2.
3.	3.
4.	4.

Commitment

    I, _____, promise to stop undermining my own success with the unhealthy habits of _____ _____,_____,_____, and ____ _____.

I will evaluate my behavior for the next three months on the following dates to be certain that I am moving in a positive direction toward my goals and dreams:

1ˢᵗ Evaluation date: _____

2ⁿᵈ Evaluation date: _____

3ʳᵈ Evaluation date: _____

The ultimate responsibility of learning to care for yourself and to give yourself permission to succeed is up to YOU. Release the ball and chain of sabotaging your own happiness and success, and embrace the wonderful feeling that you really do deserve all good things. You deserve to achieve your dreams, and it begins with your ability to care for yourself, love yourself, accept yourself, and plan for success with healthy habits.

Negative Self-Talk

Eliminate negative self-talk and vaporize self-sabotage. These are some negative self-talk beliefs that we have and find ourselves thinking or saying out loud:

- "I can't do that!"

- "I'm not good enough."

- "What makes me think that I can do it?"

- "He is too good for me."

- "I'm not a good learner."

- "I'm not smart."

- "Come on dummy, wise up!"

- "I'm so ugly."

- "If I could only lose 25 lbs."

Now let us create a self-care plan as you list daily practices that will foil your inner saboteur and develop healthy habits that will make you feel better about yourself.

Exercise

For the next seven days, write one positive statement about yourself and say the words out loud. (Say these words to yourself several times during the day. Remind yourself of what a good person you are, and that you have many strengths.)

My one week of positive statements and self-affirmations:

Day	Positive statement
1.	
2.	
3.	
4.	
5.	
6.	
7.	

In time, you will believe those affirmations, give voice to them, and be honest with your self. Truth will set you free. Believe those good things about yourself and your self-image will become healthier and more positive. Believe that you can and you will notice your words will change from "can't" and " should" to **can** and **will.** How we choose to use our gifts and talents is up to us. Break free from the bind of the past. Let the past go and live in the moment.

Exercise

What I love about myself:
1. _____
2. _____
3. _____
4. _____
5. _____

What my friends and family say are my strengths and talents:
1. _____
2. _____
3. _____

Stop comparing yourself to others. You are a unique individual with your own set of talents and skills. You are a unique individual and no one on Earth is the same as you. Be happy with who you are and recognize your talents and skills. We all fall short and make mistakes, but we can surely set goals to overcome some barriers that hold us back from enjoying our successes. Focus on the good qualities about yourself and you will begin to find the strength to deal with the unhealthy qualities. You can change the unhealthy qualities with healthy thoughts, words and habits. Talk to yourself like you were your own best friend. You want your friends to succeed, don't you? You can develop a healthy self-image and your self-care habits will replace your self-sabotage habits. Put your good qualities on an index card. Believe them, affirm them, and say them out loud. Now you have the power to change your self-image from poor to good. With a good self-image, you will practice self-care because you know that you are deserving. You will find that you no longer will have the need to subconsciously undermine all your good work and strengths. You have the ability to change your life! What are you waiting for? Now do it!

Your Prosperous Year

Wonderful! Wonderful! Fortunate me.
This is the year that my dreams come true.
This is the year that my ship comes in.
This is the year I am glad to live.
This is the year I have much to give.
This is the year when I know the truth.
This is the year I find health and new youth.
This is the year that brings happiness and joy.
This is the year I am filled with love for myself and everyone.
This is the year I will live to bless.
Wonderful! Wonderful! Fortunate me!
This is the year when all my dreams come true!

ABOUT THE AUTHOR

MARCELLA BERRY

Marcella Berry is President and CEO of Millionaire Mamaz, Inc., an exclusive organization for women, married, single, divorced or widowed who aspire to master the game of wealth. The organization introduces principles of balance and wealth in all areas of life to empower women emotional, physically spiritually, relationally and financially.

An expert on women's issues and nurse, Ms. Berry has a true passion for helping people. Ms. Berry was nominated woman of the year for Big Brothers and Big Sisters and she is a member of the International Advisory Board for the Professional Woman Network. As a Success and life coach. Ms. Berry has conducted training in the areas of Women's Issues and Diversity, Teen Image and Social Etiquette as well as Women's Wellness.

Ms. Berry also founded Successful Single Moms, a non-profit organization that provides information and resources to single moms globally. Ms. Berry is available as a keynote speaker and trainer on a national and international basis.

Contact
Marcella Berry
13547 Ventura Blvd. Suite #227
Sherman Oaks, Ca. 91423
(818) 474-7945
www.millionairemamaz.com
www.successfulsinglemomsglobalnetwork.com
Email: millionairemamaz@yahoo.com

FIVE

LIVING A MORE SIMPLE LIFE

By Marcella Berry

Today in America the pace of life can best be described as "warp speed". Some may even say it's out of control. We have twelve to sixteen-hour workdays, cellular phones attached to the ear, a barrage of emails, multiple voice mail messages, sixty seven cable channels, Saturday morning Little League games, mandatory office parties, and the list goes on and on! While the human condition thrives on mental stimulation, it also requires relaxation and a state of calm. Balance is the key to life.

It wasn't too long ago when Sunday was revered by almost everyone as a day of rest and relaxation. Stores were closed on Sunday, and families got together for Sunday dinner. There also were other days of the week, which lent themselves to periods of relaxation as well, especially in the morning or evenings after work. It was not uncommon to find people out fishing, curled up with a good book, practicing a musical instrument, or even sewing or knitting on the porch while telling stories to children. These were the days before the radio, television and the Internet. These were simple and less sophisticated times. There is something to be learned from the past: **with simplicity comes balance, and with balance comes calm.**

In thinking about simplicity as a single mom and having the demands of running a business, making business calls, responding to emails, scheduling appointments (as well as being the C.E.O of my household), having to pick the kids up from school, figuring out what to make for dinner, helping with homework, and shuttling kids to practices, I began to look at how I could live a simpler life.

What is a simpler life? It is a question I hear all the time. To live a simpler life, do I need to grow my own vegetables, recycle cans, and heat from a wooden stove? Living a simpler life will not be the same for you as it is for me. Living simple is guarding your limited time and resources.

It is also eliminating clutter and stripping away what is not important in your life, realizing that we will never get *everything* done in our daily lives. Therefore, why not slow down, prioritize in the order of importance, and enjoy the moment?

Be present in the moment and enjoy.

So you say that is easier said than done. As I stated earlier, living simple is achieved by you guarding your limited time and resources, and that is done by managing your time and setting goals. According to the late Will Rogers, "Time, like land, is your best investment because they ain't making no more of it." Time is a person's most precious investment capital. Time is valuable, and you only have so much of it. How quickly you successfully achieve your goals depends on how wisely you spend or invest it.

Do you believe that time is a precious commodity? Do you waste time? In order to stop wasting time (your success capital) you must learn how to organize your time. Before you organize your time, you must organize yourself, the very core of all personal development. People are the only living thing that are consciously aware of time, and knows that time is as finite as they are. Both the value and measurement of time is relative to each person. To a lazy person, time is valueless. It is wasted because there is too much of it and time drags. A busy person views time as a thread of gold and flies away from him. He never has enough it to accomplish what needs to be done.

The faster you move through life however, the more you will have to use. The busy person feels in constant battle for time, but by achieving more than others, you actually slow time down. The key to a balanced and successful life is better management of your time. Increasing the use of it makes it more valuable.

"Time is money", said Benjamin Franklin. Money is usually a stepping-stone to all goals in our life. Any reorganizing of time requires a plan of action. Time is saved in small bits. I am going to share with you a new program of action in 5 parts.

5 Steps to Save Time

1) Define your goals/Write down goals.

2) Set a target date for each of your goals.

3) Keep your plan realistic and workable.

4) Re-evaluate your daily routine.

5) Eliminate all non-essential activities.

Brian Tracy says if you write your goals down, you have a 100% greater chance of success completing them just by writing them down. By writing down your goals, it helps you to focus on spending your time doing those things you value, or those things that help you achieve your goals. To help you clarify your values and your long-term goals, carry out the following "thought experiment". Imagine your own funeral five years from now. What would you like people to say about you? What would you like a close friend, a member of your family, and colleague at work to say about you? The point of this exercise is not to think about your death, but about the kind of person you want to be, and the kinds of thing you wish to achieve. Five years from now is far enough away for you to do new things, but near enough not to feel remote. Don't try and guess what people would really say about you; the point of the exercise is to clarify goals and really realize what is important to you. It is good to make a personal statement of your values and goals because it helps you to center your life around what you believe in. But knowing your values and goals is not enough by itself. You need also to act in accordance with them, and that will bring on a sense of balance and simplicity. In making space for simplicity, here are some tips.

Simplicity Tips

1) Take a minute to visualize a simpler life.

2) Plan a daily ritual that will center you such as prayer, journaling, and inspirational reading.

3) Say no to something.

4) Make a list of all your commitments.

5) Break down a project you are procrastinating on to the smallest step possible.

6) Plan on the one thing you will do tomorrow—no excuse.

7) What do you enjoy about your life right now?

Chapter Summary

1) The central principle of time management is: spend your time doing those things you value or that help you achieve your goals.

2) It is important to know what your values and goals are.

3) You could clarify these by imagining what you would like people to say about you.

4) Write down your personal statement of values and goals so that you can refer to it often.

5) Having clarified your values and goals, make sure that you are led by them. Do not be led by someone else's goals.

6) Plan a daily ritual such as prayer, journaling, and inspirational reading.

7) Aim to spend as much time as possible doing those things that are important, but not urgent. This is a two step process:

- From now on, do not commit yourself to doing things that are not important

- Use the extra time this gives you to do non-urgent things. Gradually, fewer and fewer things will be urgent, because you will have done them before they are urgent.

ABOUT THE AUTHOR

SANDY SPADARO

A graduate of the Ohio State University with a fifteen year working background in sales, marketing and business management, Sandy Spadaro continues the drive toward utilizing skills in freelance writing and public speaking for multiple professional organizations through her firm, SS Marketing Solutions. Blessed with recent recognition, Spadaro has been named one of South Jersey's Top Business Women, having been showcased in the Fall 2006 issue of South Jersey Magazine, as well as having been recipient of the "Outstanding Women of Achievement 2007" for the Girl Scout's of America.

Installed as the National Association of Women Business Owners (NAWBO) -South Jersey's VP of Programs for 2006-2007, Spadaro has filled the upcoming year's calendar with value-packed education & networking functions intended to help members grow both personally & professionally. Given the importance she places on women's issues, it is of no surprise that she is active within various additional associations, including the National Association of Female Executives (NAFE) and the Professional Woman Network (PWN), playing a part in both the PWN Speaker's Bureau and the PWN Author's Institute.

Spadaro's published works have reached reader audiences through local and national publications such as Executive Female Magazine, Working Mother Magazine, Origin Magazine, Broker Agent Magazine and the Prospecting & Marketing Institute Series.

Though as a published author, public speaker and national association award winner she's committed to using her enthusiasm to provide her clients with profit through PR, she openly admits that her greatest challenge and accomplishment thus far has been that of raising her joyful and spirited 10-year old boy.

Services and events information can be found on www.ssmarketingsolutions.com.

Contact
SS Marketing Solutions
1814 Rte. 70 * Suite 350 * Beowulf Plaza
Cherry Hill, NJ 08003
856.673.4120
sandy@ssmarketingsolutions.com

SIX

COMMUNICATING YOUR FEELINGS AND NEEDS

by Sandy Spadaro

"Good communication is as stimulating as black coffee,
and just as hard to sleep after."
— Anne Morrow Lindbergh

Communication, (n.)

1. The act of transmitting;

2. The exchange of ideas and information or opinion;

3. To make known a message;

4. Synonyms; contact, consultation, interaction, transmission

Good communication can improve interactions in all aspects of personal and professional relationships. Sounds simple enough, but upon examination we find SO many ways to stray from **good** communication toward **ineffective** communication.

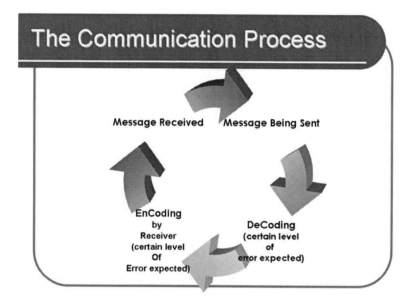

The Theory of Communication states that the cycle of expressing and understanding a message occurs at four intervals:

1. **Encoding** occurs when the sender determines *how* to send a message.

2. The sender then **conveys** the message, either verbally or nonverbally.

3. Decoding occurs when the receiver **interprets** and determines its meaning.

4. The **response** in which the receiver reacts to the sender happens last.

In any communication some of the "meaning" is lost within any one of these transmission intervals. In fact, social psychologists estimate that there is usually a 40-60% loss of message meaning between sender and receiver.

"Nothing was ever so unfamiliar and startling to me as my own thoughts."
— Henry David Thoreau

The Conversations in Our Head

The brain is on a constant mission to process the information going IN and coming OUT in order to communicate any given message at any given time. Not only do we need to consider that intended messages become lost in translation between recipients but that some of our confusions come directly from the thoughts running ramped through our own heads!

You know the drill…. someone asks a simple question, or offers a simple compliment. In the moments before our mouth opens and we form a response, the following thoughts course through the brain like a freight train:

- "I'm having a bad hair day. Why would she say I look great?"

- "Maybe she's faking it…I KNEW I couldn't trust her!"

- "Could she just be looking for a return compliment?"

- "Maybe she's buttering me up because her report is due."

- "Maybe I should blow it off…making fun of myself could be seen as humility."

- "But then I might sound insecure, and lose some of the self-confidence I'm feigning."

And so on, and so on.

What with all this converging and provocative <u>internal</u> dialogue, it's a wonder we ever get to the point where we mutter "Thank You", *truly* the only response necessary after a compliment. The point here is that, in order to understand how it is that we might better communicate with others, let's learn why we should sift through our own communication delays and roadblocks first. After all, how is anyone expected to comprehend us, when our very own messages are uncertain, ambivalent or unclear?

Why Don't We Say What We Mean?

The age-old issue of a woman's role in life is said to have begun in the garden of Adam & Eve. Beyond that, the hunting & gathering stage of our existence is where we, as women, learned to take on more than we should (what with house, home, raising children, AND work), harbor the guilt and pride that keeps us from saying "NO", and bury the skills necessary to communicate that we JUST DON'T WANT TO TAKE IT ANYMORE.

Strengthening your skill-sets in both **listening** & **assertiveness** is the foundation for ensuring that your recipient "gets" exactly what you mean, and guides the way toward continued communication.

Listening involves taking the responsibility to actively participate in receiving and "decoding" information, and is just as important, if not more so, than delivering it.

In order to effectively LISTEN to your recipient, you need to provoke material that they are willing to give you. You need to ask the "right" questions...

- "What are the challenges YOU are facing?"

- "What is the most important thing to YOU about this project?"

- "What would be your most desired outcome?"

Gaining insight into someone else's point of view, whether at home or in the boardroom, can create your ammunition and strategy for the positive outcome you're both seeking. Avoid competing for response time because you are focused on getting a turn to speak. *Always* ask for clarification when you do not understand what has been said. Additionally, the act of listening gives you the opportunity to gauge & assess the other's body language and non-verbal cues.

Non-verbal communication is comprised of several factors that are sending a message loud and clear. It's in our best interest to make sure they are sending the message we want them to.

- Visual Body Language; impatience, excitement, distaste

- Pace of speech; hurried, bored, nervous

- Tactile; hand on a shoulder=empathy, hand on a doorknob=impatience)

- Vocal tone; inquisitive, jesting, nervous, shy, flirty

Use "I" statements, rather than "You", to keep a consistent focus on the problem, and not on accusing or blaming the other person. Use facts, not judgments. Express ownership of your thoughts, feeling, and opinions. Make clear, direct, requests. They are labeled "Call to Action" statements in the marketing world, and they simply allow for the ability to tell someone what you want them to do, rather than hope or assume they will figure it out.

If You're Going to Say NO...

Superwomen, like us, must at some point say "NO", in order to avoid total burnout and overload. When that time comes, we'll need to remember two platforms from which we can dive into effective communication.

Gain control of your **emotions**, they can be a blessing. The myth that women are <u>too</u> emotional downplays the positive. Not only do emotions allow us to use heightened intuition & sensitivity, they enable us to want to help others, and appreciate when others help us. They can and should instill a sense of honesty in your message that builds trust between you and your recipient. However, emotions like anger, nervousness, and jealousy can be intense and volatile, and one must learn to harness them in order to make them work FOR you, not against you.

Organize yourself; stress is minimized when you have a game-plan, when you know how much is on your plate, and how much wiggle room there is for adding items you genuinely want to say "yes" to. When you need to explain your convictions, keep in mind that most people want one question answered first and foremost in any given communication situation… **"What's in it for me?"**

Tips for maintaining the WIIFM guideline:
- Change the way you phrase and/or begin sentences.

- Choose different words.

- Offer supporting material.

- Use graphic visuals.

- Relay real life examples.

> *"The average two-year-old is a great beacon for emotional health,*
> *displaying a full range of emotions, and*
> *moving beyond them once they are expressed."*
> — Thayler White

Scientists say that in order to keep a sharp mind and an alert attention to pertinent information, we must continually create new electrical signals (or re-use those roads less traveled) that transit through to our central nervous system. We often assume that re-stating a thought or concept will magically create a new understanding where there was no understanding before. This is not so. In fact, in order to allow your message to reach its recipient, a NEW transit may be necessary.

I. Rephrase Your Information. They're obviously not getting the point with the way you are explaining it. Though a commonly used phrase is, "Talk to me like I'm 2-years old," be aware, changing the way you phrase something does NOT mean "dummifying" it to the point of insulting one's intelligence. It may simply involve changing the words you use, or painting a mental picture as an example. [See Communication Exercises]

II: Watch Your Step. Avoid off-putting phrases, and take some measures to ensure that your conversations remain as positive as possible. Have you ever heard someone start a sentence with these phrases?

- "The way I see it…"

- "Let me tell you something…"

- "If you were smart, you would…"

- "You said…"

Think before you speak. Offer other ways to communicate a strong opinion, by beginning the sentence with a bit more diplomacy and sensitivity.

For instance, instead of saying, "The way I see it…your proposal isn't going to work"; try, "I'm not sure I understand how this proposal works." You are admitting to the responsibility of the gap in communication, but not placing blame on any one party. (Even if you don't think so. This would be the diplomacy part!) In addition, you aren't suggesting future failure of the proposal either…in fact, you are actively keeping the discussion to a current time frame, in order to maintain focus on solving your issue in the here & now. Additionally, when someone claims, "The way I see it…", they tend to be assuming that you don't ALREADY see it their way, and now you are suddenly forced into defense mode.

Ever hear this one? "If you were smart, you would tell them you have too much on your plate right now to take more on." While the messenger likely has a concerned and helpful intention, they may have just insinuated that you aren't ALREADY smart. Be cautious and aware to never, never begin telling someone your opinion by insulting theirs.

NO one likes being told what they did or didn't say, or what they did or didn't do. That's a primal trigger for the defense mechanism waiting to happen. What you might try, is keeping the conversation to YOUR OWN recollection of how the exchange of information went the first time around. For instance, "I thought I understood you to say..." or "Am I remembering correctly that you said....?" In this manner, you are allowing the individual to clarify their information *without* feeling attacked at the get-go.

Communication Exercises
A: Speak to Me In *Pictures*
Use "If, Then" statements to make visual comparisons that *paint a picture* of what you mean.

If my _____ was a (choices below), it would be _____.

- Movie

- Fruit

- Car/Motorcycle

- Flower

- Color

Example: If my work ethic was a car, it would be a Dodge RAM. Steady and classic with a great reputation.

Example: If my <u>trust</u> was a <u>flower</u>, it would be <u>an orchid</u>. It's beautiful but fragile, and needs to be handled carefully.

Example: If <u>this partnership</u> was a <u>movie</u>, it would be <u>Titanic</u>.

B: Speak to Me In *Numbers*
Get creative and rationalize with the power of numeric comparison. Gauging your information on a scale allows for the opportunity to target how hard or how soon you should be seeking to solve problems and find solutions.

On a scale of 1 to 10, my _____ is a ___.

Example: My <u>anxiety over getting the raise</u> is a <u>9</u>.

Example: My <u>nausea</u> is a <u>3</u>.

Example: My <u>impatience with the new employee</u> is a <u>7</u>.

C: Speak to Me In *Words*
Metaphors are a fantastic tool. They can force people to remain "on the same page" by suggestion and visualization in situations where your understanding of an object or concept may otherwise differ.

Use the following simple phrase anytime you need for the recipient to truly understand you with example and emotion:

My _____ is like _____ .

Example: My **<u>anger</u>** is like **<u>a red hot stove burner.</u>** I need time to cool off, but I'll still be here later, when we can talk about this again.

Example: My **frustration** is like **a train leaving the station; it starts off slowly, and increases with force & speed.** I do not feel that you met my needs earlier, and now I feel out of control.

While admittedly, you may not have a professional writer or artist's flair for the dramatic, the intention is to draw your recipient onto common ground so they can be more open to seeing your point of view.

Conflict Resolution

Resolving conflicts using communication involves awareness, consideration, and a bit of finesse. *Actions* you take will cause a direct result in the <u>reaction</u> of every person you'll encounter along your way through the passage of energy from one form to another. That's right, even scientifically; we can call it "karma".

Stay in your lane; don't confuse the issue by adding situations that either happened before, or were resolved in an undesirable way for either party in negotiation or communication.

There is no room for *judgment* in any communication. If you want to compromise and create win-win outcomes, leave judgment of someone else's style, opinion, and/or choice of words at the door.

Physically there are strategic ways to go about setting the stage for good communication, as well. When sitting at a table for discussion, place yourself at eye-level with others, either side by side or directly across. This works toward establishing a "participation level" of equality, or of parallel stature. No one gets the "head of the table", the higher seat, or the apparent upper hand. Create a non-threatening stance and maintain it through conflict banter and resolution, in order to perceive the most neutral and non-threatening environment for getting your point across.

Additional Resolution Tactics

Broken Record: Keep repeating your point without getting pulled into arguing or trying to explain yourself. Example: You need to return something, you walk into the store and say, "I decided I don't need this, and I'd like my money back." Then, no matter what the clerk says, you keep repeating, "I decided I don't need this, and I'd like my money back." Avoid manipulation, baiting, and irrelevant logic.

Screening: Agree with as much of the conversation facts as you want to, but don't agree to change your stance. This method helps you avoid argument and criticism. Example: *Them:* "The proposal is awfully short, don't you think you should revise it to include more? *You:* "Thanks, you're right, it is rather short, just as I'd intended it to be."

Summarization: Make sure you have understood the other person, and give them an opportunity to correct you if you're wrong. Example: "So what you're trying to tell me is ...." or "What I heard you say was...."

Specificity: Prevent distractions by being very clear about what you want done (the Call to Action). Example: "The thing I really want is for you to change the toilet paper roll when it's empty."

How Well Do We Communicate In Written Form?

Let's take a few moments to think about how we can further strategize if we decide to send our messages via the written word. There are 3 general reasons why e-communication can falter:

1. Emails lack non-verbal cues like facial expression & tone of voice.

2. The pressure to send immediate responses can lead to carelessness.

3. The inability to build personal rapport creates sensitivity to conflict.

The following guidelines are worth taking a few minutes to exercise prior to sending ANY electronic communications, whether business or personal.

E-Communication Tips & Tactics

- RE-read ALOUD before pressing send.

- Revise where necessary.

- Exercise proper use of spelling & grammar.

- Get a second opinion (proofreader) when possible.

- Remember that you're still conducting business.

- No ambiguous terminology.

- Have a great signature file including ALL your contact information.

- Know thy receiver (otherwise you are spamming).

- Make material timely & useful.

- Follow the "Short Attention Span" premise; get your point across succinctly.

Summary

Before any communication, ask yourself a few standard questions about your messaging, whether verbal or written.

- If I were hearing this message, how would I react?

- Am I giving my recipient a precise "call to action"?

- Have I outlined a win-win situation?

- Are my emotions in check and my phrasing assertive?

- Have I left all criticism and judgment at the door?

- Is there a more visual way to get my point across?

- Have I double-checked grammar, punctuation and spelling?

The point where communication is effective, concise, and of benefit to each party involved is, in most cases, a learned skill and not a natural talent. In fact, I'd venture to call this success a "verbal homerun", because it takes practice, hard work and enthusiasm. And when the homerun has been scored, you have a new understanding and respect of the team members that shared the experience with you. At that point, motivation may increase, negotiations might occur, and goals can be met.

It just doesn't get much better than that.

Recommended Reading

Coping with Difficult People by Robert M.Bramson, New York: Anchor/ Doubleday, 1981

Self-Assertion for Women by Pamela Butler, San Francisco, CA: Harper & Row, 1981.

When I Say No, I Feel Guilty by Manual J. Smith, New York: The Dial Press, 1975.

You Just Don't Understand by Deborah Tannen, PhD., New York: Ballantine Books, 1984.

Internet Resources

www.Understandmen.com

www.psychologyhelp.com

www.creatingwe.com

Resources

A Handout on Assertiveness by Vivian Barnette, Ph.D, University of Iowa, September 5, 2000.

That's Not What I Meant by Deborah Tannen, PhD., New York: Ballantine Books, 1986.

Between Trapezes Flying into a New Life with the Greatest of Ease by Gail Blanke, Rodale, 2004.

Be Your Own Therapist by Thayler White, MA MFCC. Online Publication, www.helpself.com/thayer.htm

The Power to Connect by Theresa Easler and Chuck Easler, Motivated Publishing Ventures, 2003.

ABOUT THE AUTHOR

MERCEDES SUSANA PAGLILLA DE VAZ PITALUGA

Mercedes Pitaluga is BM University Analyst, and Languages, Sciences and Technology teacher for second graders in Potomac, Maryland. Having pursued University credits in French Literature at Palermo University in her homeland Buenos Aires, Mrs. Pitaluga specialized in Foreign Languages holding several certifications including British Cultural of London Buenos Aires, British Council Singapore, Chambre de Commerce et d'Industrie de Paris and Brazilian-Argentinean Center from Brazil and Argentina. Having shown special interest in writing, she is certified as Free-lance writer for newspapers and magazines by the Montgomery College. Her previous published works include a Theoretical-Pedagogical work written in Portuguese and registered at the National Library, Ministry of Culture Rio de Janeiro Brazil.

She has had ten years of experience conducting Ceremonial and Etiquette for women, youth,and Public Ministries and Universities from such countries as Argentina, Brazil, Chile, Venezuela, Singapore, China, Malaysia, USA, Columbia, Bolivia, Peru and India. She is a lecturer, speaker, makeup artist, educator and consultant.

Mrs. Pitaluga would like to dedicate this chapter to her mother Dr. Susana Aurora Rodriguez de Paglilla, her "Big architect" and to Mrs Lidis Bosetti de Buguñá.

Contact
www.pro-mujerplus.com
www.protrain.net
www.fountaininstitute.com

SEVEN

9 STEPS TO HIGHER SELF-ESTEEM

By Mercedes Paglilla

Why nine steps, you wonder? Why not ten, fifteen, or even fifty? When one thinks of the number nine, one automatically feels that there is something missing. Wouldn't we all feel more comfortable with the perfect number ten? The use of nine steps is no oversight, as it is precisely the discomfort in not reaching ten that illustrates the core element of a fulfilling program toward heightened self-esteem. It is only when you are continually striving to upgrade your goals, your life, and your internal view of yourself, that true and profound self-esteem can be achieved. Let's journey through the nine steps together.

In working toward better self-esteem, there are three elements at play:

- Emotions

- "Glasses" (or perspective)

- Life facts

Each of these components will be used together in an exercise called: "mind stepping" that is an intellectual workout program of 9 steps toward improved self-esteem.

First, let's take a moment to look at the fundamentals with which we will be working.

Emotions

We talk about emotions all of the time, but what are they really, and how do they influence our sense of self? Just as we may use our arms and legs to stay balanced on a beam, our emotions are in constant interplay to allow us to reach equilibrium in our minds. Let's take the strong emotion of fear as an example. When one fears a situation, this emotion is not only a reaction, but also an instrument to protect oneself. It works with existing feelings to guide our behavior and to create our sense of self at that precise moment, and also in the future.

"Glasses"

Glasses are another way of talking about how we perceive external input and how we translate it for our internal world. (We have all heard the expression, "She looks at the word through 'rose colored glasses'!)

Life Facts

Facts are those components of your life that are a part of your biography. Some of these facts can change over time, such as marital status, health condition, and financial security. Other facts, such as age, race, ethnicity, and loss of loved ones, are out of our control, and are unchangeable. These facts together comprise our personal history. During the course of our lives, we must accept these facts, and learn to manage the changes in these facts as they occur.

Working With the Nine Steps

Using the fundamentals of self-esteem described, we can now start our exercise of "mind stepping" to systematically train the mind to process our surrounding experiences in a different way. We can think of it as a kind of intellectual workout toward reaching a profound sense of self-esteem.

The program of mind-stepping can be visualized as a ladder, wherein one must start and complete each step before moving on to the next level. Each step builds the foundations for achievement of the next.

Illustrated by Aaron Camper

Step 1: Getting to Know Yourself—The Yes/No Test for Breaking Predictability.

One exercise that can be helpful in getting started in knowing yourself is the yes/no test.

This test is designed to help you break old habits, and know predictable ways of feeling.

As with any other repair work, one must first conduct an assessment of the current state of affairs.

Habits	Yes/No
Do you recognize your own negative behavioral patterns when facing changes, transition and unexpected turns?	
Do you manage to control emotions in the face of a highly stimulating situation?	
Would you feel afraid?	
Would you feel angry?	
Would you recognize your very first defensive attitude when confronting frustration?	

Step 2: The Cold -Very Cold Shower

"If you don't change your approach,
all the persistence in the world will never pay off."
— Anthony Robbins

In this step, the objective is to stop calling attention to negative behaviors and actually take action to change them. First off, it is important to kick procrastination patterns, which leads to emotional malaise, mild stress, and chronic irritability.

"When we postpone, delay and avoid timely
and relevant activities we procrastinate. "
— Dr William J. Knaus

Depending on the intensity of your procrastination, you may even be partaking in escapist behaviors, such as not answering the telephone, overly socializing, and even watching television. Procrastination is a natural reaction when one feels overwhelmed by a particular task. However, extended or chronic procrastination leaves you completely immobilized and in a poor state, as you are continuously uncomfortable and guilty about the very task that you are not doing.

Step 3: Setting Up Your Program Package

This step involves an exercise that will prepare you to alter some of the self-destructive behaviors listed above. Here is what you will need:

- A yellow covered journal (You can also write down in the space provided.)

- A pencil

- Some amulets and lucky charms, including <u>one cherished photo of yourself</u> (important!), one letter from a loved one, and one piece of music that you particularly enjoy.

These tools will be used to start establishing links and connections with the past and the present.

Now that you have your tools, we'll need to focus on positive thoughts in order to heal past wounds. The use of positive memories can be very instrumental in bringing up inner energy for this process. Let's start.

Step 4: Walking the Ladder

"...The shift in mental posture aligns you more precisely with your goals. Once you decide that something is a priority, you give it tremendous emotional intensity, and any resource that supports its attainment will eventually become clear..."
— Anthony Robbins

Illustrated by Aaron Camper

Exercise

• **Grade 1 – Awareness:** In this grade, you begin to make the first connections between you and the events around you. At this point, you may feel some discomfort, but this can be a positive signal, as discomfort can be terribly informative about areas of your life that need repair.

Practical Task: Pick up your chosen photo. We'll need to focus on positive thoughts, and fill the wounds with your positive memories from where we'll pick up inner energy. Let's start. Look at your photo, that smiling face, recovering the sensation of happiness and fulfillment. Yes, it's you! Think of a wonderful time that occurred during that period of time in your life. Close your eyes and feel the memory.

- **Grade 2 – Reliving Your Negative Memories:** Some of the hardest things to relive are bad memories. However, in this grade, you will externalize these memories, and document them as a way to look at them more objectively.

Practical Task: Pick up your yellow journal and start writing. This won't be an easy task. Think of a comment or situation that occurred during the period of time when that photo was taken. What happened? What is one word that would describe your feelings after that incident? How can you look at that more objectively, and consider why someone hurt you or your feelings?

_____

_____

- **Grade 3 – Changing Roles:** In this grade, you will play the role of the "devil's advocate" in looking at the negative memories documented in the previous grade. Let us presume that this person was right in their comment. You can simply "surf the waves", or just let the comment go and keep it outside of yourself. If you let the comment take undo importance, it ends up being your own internal voice that is repeating the negative comment to yourself. This, in turn, creates negative and self-destructive feelings. So, don't fight against it, just let it go.

Practical Task: wear your "dark glasses" and play "devil's advocate". Why did this person treat you unkindly, or say cruel words? What was happening in their life that would cause them to be unkind?

- **Grade 4 – Identifying Yourself in Society:** In this grade, you will take a closer look at how you are in the world. Forget emotional matters or your own internal labels for now and focus on the basics of who you are from an external point of view. Who are you in regard to society as whole? Mother? Wife? American? South American? Christian? Muslim? Political or Non-Political? Volunteer? Daughter? Friend? Businesswoman?

Practical Task: write down the different external identifications of yourself here or in your yellow journal.

- _____
- _____
- _____
- _____
- _____
- _____
- _____

- **Grade 5 – Accepting Yourself and Linking to Others**: If you've been experiencing a very difficult time in life and there something you feel guilty of, let it go! "Change that skin" and let it go. Forgive yourself, and if someone else has hurt you in the past, forgive them.

Step 5: Affirmations

Shaping our beliefs by our style of communication. List below sentences that describe who you are with positive, verb-oriented words.

1. _____

2. _____

3. _____

What is one verb-oriented word that describes you perfectly?

1. _____

Step 6: From Ordinary to Extraordinary

We program our mental rehearsal with the first sound we hear at birth: **Our Name.** Think back to when you were a child, when you heard your parents call your name. Did it make you feel warm and loved? Or were you oftentimes criticized and punished? As an adult, are you proud of your name and who you are?

Exercise:

Go to a stationary shop or office supply store and buy some white stickers. Write your name on each of these stickers, and place a positive action verb that describes you on each sticker. Place these stickers around your house (bathroom mirror, refrigerator, etc). Also, place successes that you have achieved under your name.

Learn to be proud of your name and who you are. Remind yourself that you are not ordinary, but EXTRAORDINARY.

Write your name and what comes to mind when you think of it:

1. _____
2. _____
3. _____

Step 7: Stay Inspired. Look for Your Role Model

Try to find someone in your mastery or interest area to be your mentor. How did they achieve their goals? What obstacles did they overcome? They achieved their goals when they aligned them to their dreams. They imagined themselves achieving their goals, not only the image, but the feeling, the anticipation of the sensation of already being THERE. That gave them a tremendous empowerment to shape their belief system exactly towards their goals...

Step 8: On Your Mark! Get Set! Go!

Affirmations are a wonderful way to lift your self-esteem. Circle all the words that best describe you, and say each word aloud as you circle it. (Write extra descriptive words in the blank boxes, if you have other words that really describe you.)

Caring	Energized	Avoids Stress	Communicator
Dancer	Warm	Kind	Outgoing
Charismatic	Loving	Intelligent	Organized
Good Parent	Faithful Friend	Dynamic	Athletic
Fun	Patient	Goal Setter	Kind
Loves Animals	World Traveler	Embrace Differences	Educated
Daring	Spiritual	Creative	Healthy Lifestyle

Step 9: Make Room for Mindfulness

Listen to what you tell yourself about success—the real inner message. Are you telling yourself you should be a hero in all fields, always sustaining gains and leaving worries behind? Pin the idea down. Clarify it. In what area are you trying TOO hard and attempting the impossible?

In what areas are you trying **too hard,** and never really feeling satisfied or successful?

1. _____

2. _____

3. _____

Figure out why this line of thought is self-defeating. Then get skeptical about this false logic. Keep applying a reasoned skepticism until you can no longer find a reason to believe the unreasonable. Be forever mindful about the way you talk to yourself, and how you really define success. Set **attainable** goals for yourself, and learn to "Let Go and Let God" in many areas of your life.

Whatever your faith, allow God to be your endless source of inner energy, your life fuel. May you find these nine steps helpful in building stronger self-esteem, and knowing yourself in a better way.

ABOUT THE AUTHOR

MICKI K. JORDAN, MLDR

 Micki Kremenak Jordan is a mentor, trainer and coach. She has held a variety of management positions over the past twenty-five years. She has participated on Visioning and Strategic Planning Teams and is currently a member of the Leadership Development Team for Providence Presbyterian Church.

Ms. Jordan has a Bachelor of Science Degree in Sociology from the University of Iowa. After several years in the corporate world she obtained her Masters of Arts in Leadership in 2001 from Bellevue University. Ms. Jordan is certified in Diversity Training, Public Speaking and Professional Coaching. She holds the Certified Insurance Councilor Designation and is a member of the Professional Woman Network (PWN) and the National Association of Female Executives (NAFE).

Her passion is assisting others to recognize their true potential. Her plans for the future include developing and presenting small group seminars for college students and upwardly mobile career women. She also plans on doing more writing.

Contact
Micki K. Jordan
11066 Rodeo Circle
Parker, CO 80138
(720) 851-6964
mickijordan@yahoo.com

EIGHT

SUPER VISION

By Micki Jordan

"Shoot for the Moon! Even if you miss, you'll still be among the stars."
— Les Brown

Superwoman may be any woman who is attempting to multi-task her way through life. If you are anything like me, (and you must be if you are reading a book about *Overcoming the Superwoman Syndrome),* the extent of your vision is getting through the day. Many of you use a planner to keep track of activities. Included in that planner are places to create your "To Do's", that list of places to go, people to see, and things that must be done over the next day, the next week, and possibly the next month. The problem may be that you are living day-to-day, week-to-week, or month-to-month, without real direction as to where you are headed. Who is really in control of your life?

It is time to take personal responsibility for your life, for the direction you are going and for where you plan to end up. We cannot continue to wait for the right moment to take time to define our real purpose for life, or continue to think it will become laid out in front of us. Only YOU have the ability to determine what you want out of life. Earl Nightingale said, "People with goals succeed because they know where they are going. It is as simple as that."

Purpose

In order to determine your goals, you must first have a vision. In order to develop that vision, it helps to find your purpose. Some people are born with knowing what their purpose is in life. They just "know" what they are meant to do with their lives. I would guess the majority of us do not fall in that category. We may pursue a number of things without finding any real satisfaction. We may also discover a purpose along the way, but how do we know if it is "OUR" purpose.

In order to define what your main or central mission of life might be, let us look at three areas. The goal is to find an overlapping or interconnection between these areas. For each of these you will make a list. The areas are your (1) **Talents, Skills, and Abilities**, (2) your **Interests**, and (3) your **Passions**. Under your **Talents, Skills, and Abilities,** list all of the things you are good at, and that come easily for you. Are you an expert in anything, hold a degree, or have specific training, or have specialized knowledge? These may include communication skills, analytical ability, creativity, physical skills and ability, musical, interpersonal, intrapersonal, or being able to identify the relationship between things, seeing the big picture. Next, list your **Interests,** those things that you would like to learn or know more about. What might spark your curiosity? If you could become an expert in a certain field, what would it be? (This area should focus on intellectual interests.) The last list includes your **Passions.** This includes the things you enjoy doing, what gets you excited. What things do you feel strongly about? Are there things you have always wanted to try, but never have?

Identify Your:

Talents, Skills, & Abilities	Interests	Passions

Once you have completed your lists of your Talents, Skills, and Abilities, Interests, and Passions, look at your lists and determine what interconnects. Highlight or circle the areas that appear on each list. List out the areas of interconnection; there should be at least three to six of them. These areas will be used as a directional basis for creating your vision. List the interconnections here: (These just may provide an "Aha!" moment.)

Vision

In order to begin creating a vision statement, we need to look at what a vision is.

Vision is:
- Concentrating on the future
- Built on the Past
- Clear
- Inspiring
- Based on Reality
- Insightful
- Detailed
- Empowering
- Challenging
- Customized
- Dreaming the possible Dream
- Strategic
- Long Term
- Coming from God

The purpose of developing a vision statement is to define what is possible, to inspire, energize and motivate your creativity, to use your imagination to see things as they can be in your life. Albert Einstein said, "Imagination is more powerful than knowledge." Knowledge allows us to see things as they are; imagination is necessary to see things as we would like them to be. It is important to remember that imagination is not just dreams, it is a vision based on reality, based on your **Talents, Skills, Abilities, Passions and Interests.** As you become more aware of what is possible, your life will become more focused and fulfilling.

Creating

You are now ready to create vision statements. I am recommending you create a statement for where you want to be in five years, in ten years, and at retirement. Other crossroads that deserve a vision statement could include: as children grow up, as they reach high school, college, or leave home. These all create situations that are changes in your life. Using your defined areas of purpose, create statements that will give your life direction and meaning. Remember, these statements need to have the elements defined in the Vision section discussed previously. Make the statements personal and in the present tense; keep them simple, clear, and brief. An example of a possible five-year vision statement is: "I will graduate with a Master's Degree involving Organizational Development." Now it is your turn. Review your areas of purpose, use your imagination, and remember the sky is the limit.

My 5-Year Vision:	
My 10-Year Vision:	
Retirement Vision:	

Goals

The final step in creating your Super Vision is to set some goals. These are necessary in order to complete your Vision. The hardest part is finished, because you have determined your visions, but now there needs to be a path to achieve those visions. Without the goals, your visions will only become dreams; they will not be fulfilled. As you set your goals, they must contain several key elements. Goals must be:

- **Specific** – What you want to accomplish, stated in the positive.

- **Measurable in some way** – It identifies the difference of where you are now to where you want to be.

- **Inspirational** – Something you really want, even if in the short term you have to do things that are not necessarily "pleasurable".

- **Unconditional** – Simple, present tense, and in the affirmative. I will achieve it.

- **Written down and reviewed regularly** – It brings commitment.

- **Realistic** – You must know clearly what you want to achieve.

My Goals Are:	Potential Obstacles:

Visualize:

Once you have completed your goals, visualize what will take place. This visualization will set the goals in your mind, it will make things clear, and they will become more a part of you. You will be able to close your eyes and see what it will look like when your visions come to life. You will be able to "feel" the pleasure of accomplishing what is important to you, fulfilling you life. John Atkinson said, "If you don't run your own life, someone else will." Do you want someone else running your life? I think not. Embrace your Super Visions and make them real.

Your Dimension Of Greatness
No one can know the potential,
Of a life that is committed to win;
With courage - the challenge it faces,
To achieve great success in the end!
So, explore the Dimension of Greatness,
And believe that the world CAN be won;
By a mind that is fully committed,
KNOWING the task can be done!
Your world has no place for the skeptic,
No room for the DOUBTER to stand;
To weaken your firm resolution
That you CAN EXCEL in this land!
We must have VISION TO SEE our potential,
And FAITH TO BELIEVE that we can;
Then COURAGE TO ACT with conviction,
To become what GOD MEANT us to be!
So, possess the strength and the courage,

To conquer WHATEVER you choose;
It's the person WHO NEVER GETS STARTED,
That is destined FOREVER to lose!
— Author Unknown

Notes:

_____

_____

_____

_____

_____

_____

_____

_____

_____

_____

_____

_____

_____

_____

_____

_____

_____

_____

_____

_____

_____

ABOUT THE AUTHOR

VALERIE FLEMING

Valerie Fleming is President and CEO of Thyme4Tax, *The Season for Your Business*. Specializing in business coaching and finance management, Valerie helps entrepreneurs cultivate new business and fosters life into existing business. Her continuous support of customized programs helps to guide young seedlings into a fully grown tree able to withstand the seasonal change of business.

With over twenty-five years in the tax and finance industry Valerie has the unique ability to be compassionate yet objective. Valerie has coached existing businesses through significant growth surges by utilizing fundamental building blocks already in place. "We bridge system gaps to maximize employee productivity and promote oneness and success within the organization", says Valerie, "everyone benefits".

A company wide layoff from Tratec/McGraw Hill inspired Valerie to form "The Accounting Connection", a tax and accounting service for individuals and small business. Despite personal challenges, impassioned and committed Valerie steered her new business through a then tough, lean California economy. After relocating to New York, she accepted a leadership position with The Hudson River Foundation, but continued pursuing her dream of one day running a successful business. In keeping with her entrepreneurial spirit, that day eventually came to fruition after serving resignation to an Ohio employer, and subsequently launching "Thyme4tax". Valerie maintains an office both in New York and Ohio.

Through her affiliation with Professional Woman Network (PWN), she has obtained the following certifications: Marketing a Consulting Practice, and Women's Issues and Diversity. She has co-author of *"You're on Stage! Branding, Image and Style"*. Valerie is a member of NAFE, and is a Certified QuickBooks Pro Advisor.

Contact
Valerie Fleming
P.O. Box 201836
Shaker Heights, OH 44120
216-991-8994
216-991-6096 fax
516-521-3298 cell
tyme4tax@scbglobal.net
www.protrain.net

NINE

OVERCOMING OBSTACLES, TRANSITION AND CHANGE

By Valerie Fleming

The very notion of having to "**overcome**" something, gain the mastery of, prevail over, is a formidable, yet somber thought. In most cases, the onus is on **you** to make changes. On the other hand, to be "**overcome**" with pity, or to be made helpless, is generally preceded by an event of which you have absolutely no control. In each scenario, however, your life has been modified, and the need has arisen to "Overcome Obstacle, Transition and Change" both professionally and personally. Our professional and personal lives are closely entwined. How we deal with an employment setback can be closely linked with how we handle a troubled marriage, which in turn affects how we deal with an employment setback. Do we feel equipped to move forward effectively? Is there a formula to move forward successfully? Can we "**overcome**" The Superwoman Syndrome and still feel wanted, needed, appreciated, respected without losing ourselves within the process? This chapter is designed to remove the paralyzing fear that can either mutate or prevent change. Change can pave the way to proactive accomplishment, an embracement of the unknown. "Given time and baring occurrences", you are in control of what happens next. Through out this text I will intermittingly refer to Obstacle, Transition and Change as "Challenges".

I often give thought to how some individuals are able to quickly assess their challenge, execute a plan of survival, and effortlessly continue in life without ever looking back. Others, while just as tenacious, need "me time" and are more reflective. They examine, dissect and internalize every facet of each challenge. Once the challenge is worked out, decisions are made, and life goes on. Yet others struggle, feel every bump in the road - similar to the "slow stochastic" stock market indicator - rarely seek advice, and marginally get through each day. Challenge is never addressed. Change seldom occurs. Personal or professional success is rarely met.

Can you identify yourself in any of the three patterns above? As you become the professional woman, you must scrutinize how you deal with challenge. Determine if your method is effective, or if it in fact sabotages your progress. As a professional, you will be faced with countless assessments that test your core being. You must learn to meet these challenges quickly, effectively, with poise and diplomacy. Not every challenge will be overwhelming or negative; some challenges will be presented as gifts. Tucked inside each overt challenge and each subtle gift are building blocks that will provide you with resilience to meet the next. Benefit is derived only if you are prepared, and have developed a healthy perspective of challenge. To prepare for this journey, you must first know where you are and where you need to be.

Identify Your Value

Values represent the measure used to make decisions. Values rouse us to overcome challenge. Values allow us to set priorities reflecting what we regard as being most important. If you want something bad enough, you have the ability to *align the mind to fit the will*. We have the gift of free moral agency to choose values, and are held accountable for our actions by others and ourselves.

Exercise 1

Using the matrix following, first identify your value – what is most important to you; read to the right to ascertain the challenge. Use blank areas to write in your value that may not be listed. Values may be "regrouped" according to the type of challenge you perceive them to be in your life. Remember this is *your* personal exercise designed to help *you* identify *your* value, to focus on what you truly aspire to, then determine the challenge that stands between you and that goal. Stay mindful of *your* values, as you will utilize them in subsequent exercises throughout this chapter.

Chart (A)

Value	Challenge	Definition
Education Opportunity Self Esteem Time Management	Obstacle	Anything that impedes one from moving forward.
Promotion Relocation Change in Marital Status	Transition	A passing from one situation or place to another.
Lifestyle Belief System Discipline	Change	To become distinctly different, altered or, transformed.

Keeping your personal challenge(s) in mind from exercise 1, consider the experiences below that reveal how three different individuals of diverse cultural backgrounds faced challenge and executed a plan of action. Notice the outcome of each (My personal experience is sited in challenge #2 and #3).

1. Obstacle:

"Of course, I am resolved to rise above every obstacle, but how will it be possible?" said Beethoven, one of the greatest classical composers of symphony. Beethoven depended on his innate gift, his internal rhythm, his "ear" to create timeless concerto. One of the most famous things about Beethoven as a person was his deafness. It is hard to imagine being able to compose music as wonderful as the Choral Symphony, while being unable to hear the music except in one's head. Once Beethoven was encouraged to help conduct at a rehearsal for the Choral Symphony. Even as the rehearsal finished, Beethoven was still conducting to the orchestra, and he had to be made aware that the musicians had finished playing. Beethoven continued composing twenty-one years after going deaf. A profound example of overcoming obstacles!

2. Transition:

At the reluctance of my parents, in my late teens, alone, with determination, $100 in my pocket, and an army trunk containing all of my then known belongings, I transitioned from the safe, nurturing "nest" called home in Ohio to life on the West Coast. No employment, not even a prospect. Home became a downtown Los Angeles YWCA room, which was paid up for one week, no friends and no then known relatives. My value was relocation to explore life on a grander scale, but in doing so I moved away from my support system of family and friends. It is easy to be strong and make wise decisions when surrounded by fortification. The transition left me vulnerable. That vulnerability led to many, many trials, heartbreaks and disappointments. However, as a result I learned self trust, intuitiveness, and developed whole strength. For the next twenty years I remained on the West Coast, developed a secular niche, made lifetime friends, attended college and married. The *scores* of challenges I encountered during that period were fundamental to professional and personal growth. To this very day I continue to draw from that transition.

3. Change:

My friend "Gloria", from a broken home, determined to provide her five children with a quality of life she never had, and made sacrifices to make this happen. Gloria and her husband determined that she would stay home to provide constant care for the children while he worked. When the marriage failed, Gloria suffered a nervous breakdown, which eventually lead to estrangement from all five of her children. We lost contact; years passed until one day, en-route to an appointment, I ran into Gloria. We embraced; I immediately recognized the voice but not the person, as she looked completely different. The trauma in her personal life changed her entire being; it completely altered the person I once knew.

Did all meet challenge effectively? Would you conclude that experience #1 and #2 triumphed while experience #3 failed? What if the circumstances were switched between the three individuals, would the outcome have been the same? We will never be able to assess that scenario with precision. However, armed with definitive facts about ourselves, owning up to both our strengths and struggles, we can face potential challenges with a measure of accuracy, shift gears, and implement a plan of action so as not to "strike the air".

Assess Your Strengths and Weaknesses

Self-evaluation is essential to overcoming challenges. Reflect deeply on pivotal periods in your life. Be honest, regardless of how uncomfortable this process of self-assessment can be. Indicate strengths you possess that were instrumental during this period, and weakness that impeded growth. Before engaging in exercise 2, 3 and 4, refer back to exercise 1 where you have identified your value and associated challenge(s).

Exercise 2

List the obstacles in your life that have prevented growth:

1.
2.
3.
Strengths:
Weakness:

Exercise 3

List transitional periods in your life that have challenged your comfort zone:

1.
2.
3.
Strengths:
Weakness:

Exercise 4

List changes to your life that have modified your core person:

1.
2.
3.

Strengths:
Weakness:

From each exercise, what feelings are dominant? Anger? Vengeance? Fear? Self-Defeat? Hurt? Self-Pity? Bitterness? What values from childhood have been programmed, shape who you are, and need to be changed? It takes courage to be honest. Enlist the opinion of a friend who knows you well, cares about you, and who will be an objective evaluator. Do not sabotage this exercise by discounting corrective feedback.

Exercise 5
List dominant self-defeating feelings that need to be eradicated:

1.
2.
3.
4.
5.

If you listed anger, hurt, or fear in exercise 5, keep in mind that those feelings serve a dual purpose: They can have a negative effect, but eventually serve as strong, positive motivational tools. Remove other feelings that leave you powerless and unmotivated.

Chart (B)

Beliefs	Motivator	Non-Motivator	Dominant Feelings
I will find a solution to my immediate problem.	X		Optimism, Confidence
I will never be able to grow in this company.		X	Despair, Hopelessness, Depression
I'd like to launch my new business, but what if I fail?		X	Pessimism, Uselessness, Fear
Management is forcing me out of this company that I have worked so hard to build, but a career change may bring me closer to my professional goal.	X		Fear, Anger, Hurt, Optimism
Be careful whom you talk to around here, they might use it against you.		X	Fear, Anger, Distrust

Always question yourself. "What is my need?" "What is my objective?" "What do I want to accomplish?" Addressing these questions aids you in feeling less overwhelmed and more in control of your situation, so that a plan of action can be developed.

Embrace Your Challenge

Earlier in this chapter, change was defined as "to become distinctly different, altered or transformed". Think about that; who wants to be completely different or altered venturing off to the unknown, pioneering the unpaved path? It is a frightening thought indeed. However, each period of life requires change in order to grow. On the other hand, fear averts the risk of change. When we stay in our comfort zone and hold on to self-defeating feelings, we move backwards, because we loose confidence and sense of worth. We ask ourselves, "Why am I so weak?" "Why am I so afraid to do that?" Those thoughts alone perpetuate fear. For years we remain comfortable, to others we appear inept.

While embracing change, an appropriate degree of concern is necessary to avoid mistakes. Try not to underestimate or overestimate risks. If deciding to leave a lucrative position to venture out on your own, consider the following:

- Have a contingency plan in place.

- Six months savings to replace lost income is the rule of thumb until your venture takes off.

- Tell yourself, "Yes, I see the problems, but I don't want to miss out on the opportunities."

- Ask yourself, "What will happen to growth, my potential, and me if I don't pursue this course?"

- Seek win–win solutions. The Superwoman tends to seek the benefit of others, while discounting her own. Eliminate the unhealthy win–lose option.

It is impossible to contemplate every single risk, twist, and turn, as we journey into a new direction. However, we are able to embrace change if proper measures are taken. We plan for the known. It is the unknown that mutates plan.

Exercise 6

What do you want to accomplish, both professionally and personally, in one to five years?

1.
2.
3.
4.
5.

Exercise 7

What could prevent your plans from taking place?

1.
2.
3.
4.
5.

Exercise 8

What strategies do you have in place to deal with each possible deterrent?

1.
2.
3.
4.
5.

Exercise 9

How can you utilize your strengths to achieve your desired accomplishments?

1.	
2.	
3.	
4.	
5.	

Chart Your Progress

After having unwrapped and exposed longtime, delicate areas of your life to yourself and others, conclude that portion of your journey with an evaluation of your personal inventory. Carefully review the chart below and truthfully rate each area on a scale of 1 to 10 with 10 being the strongest, and 1 being the weakest. Utilize blank areas to write in your personal inventory that may not be listed. Begin with how you feel *this* day, and place that date under the column marked "**Current**", under which you will rate each area listed. Closely track your progress, with reassessment in six-month time increments.

Chart (C)

Your Personal Inventory	Current	In Six Months	In Twelve Months
DATE			
Drive, Determination, Passion			
Knowledge in Your Area of Expertise			

Effective Written and Verbal Communication			
Positive Outlook			
Self-Confidence			
Mental, Emotional Flexibility			
Support System (family, friends, mentor)			
Strong Spiritual Values			
Rest, Healthy Diet and Exercise			
Organizational Skills			
Self-Help (books, seminars)			
TOTAL			

Total column and refer to rating system below for self-evaluation.

Chart (D)

RATING SYSTEM				
100	-	90	Excellent	Mentor others. Develop a team of professionals.
89	-	80	Good	Continue growing. Strengthen your personal niche.
79	-	50	Need Improvement	Hone in on weaknesses. Solicit frank feedback.
49	-	25	Poor	Rid Negatives, prioritize, and seek professional help.

When life turns a page and you never give up, amazing things can happen. Therefore, develop a place in your soul that is sacred to you and you alone. You will visit that place repeatedly, as you walk through life. As stated at the outset of this chapter, you are in control of what happens next. Do not simply peer at challenge. Face it. Embrace it. Take your pain and turn it into power.

References

"Of course, I am resolved to rise above every obstacle, but how will it be possible?"
—Johann Sebastian Bach:
www.classicalcomposerbiographies.com

Recommended Reading

Making Change Irresistible by Ken Hultman

The Procrastinator's Guide to Success by Lynn Lively

Discovering Your Personality Type by Don Richard Riso and Russ Hudson

Notes:

_____

_____

_____

_____

_____

_____

_____

_____

_____

_____

_____

_____

_____

_____

_____

_____

_____

_____

_____

_____

_____

_____

ABOUT THE AUTHOR

Terri Tibbs

Terri Tibbs, President of Tibbs & Associates Consulting Group, is a certified trainer and coach and a member of the Professional Woman Network (PWN). Her seminars and workshops are designed to provide individuals with the necessary stimuli that motivates them to take action, discover potential, embrace change and seize opportunities.

She has over twenty years experience in the field of Human Resources management, Facilitation, Coaching and Acquisition Integration. She has a Bachelor's degree in Psychology from N.C. A&T State University and a Masters Degree in Human Resources Management from S.U.N.Y, Binghamton.

She has served on a number of Boards, including PWN International Advisory Board, Girl Scouts of America (Illinois Crossroads Council), Shepherd's Gate Hospice, TSOD Church Advisory Board and the United Way Allocations.x

In addition, to the Superwoman Syndrome, she will be serving as co-Author for the forthcoming books: *A Woman's Survival Guide for Obstacles, Transition & Change,* and *Women as Leaders: Strategies for Empowerment & Communication*

Contact
Tibbs & Associates Consulting Group
P.O. Box 8167
Gurnee, IL 60031
(847) 543-9380
Tibbsassociates@hotmail.com
www.protrain.net

TEN

TURNING DREAMS INTO REALITY

By Terri Tibbs

A Dream is a wish your heart makes
When you're fast asleep.
In dreams you lose your heartaches.
Whatever you wish for, you keep.

Have faith in your dreams and someday
Your rainbow will come smiling thru.
No matter how your heart is grieving,
If you keep on believing,
The dream that you wish will come true.

— Linda Ronstadt, Disney Wishes CD

Reflection

Reflect for a moment on one of your dreams that came true. What did you do to turn that dream into a reality? What obstacles did you have to overcome?

Now reflect on one of your dreams that has not yet been realized. What are the things that are preventing you from turning that dream into a reality?

Attributes of a Dream

Too often, we approach our dreams in a magical, mystical manner, thinking that they just happen by themselves. We embrace a fairy tale mentality. I believe dreams have many dimensions and properties. This chapter explores dreams from this very different perspective.

Precious – Dreams are like precious jewels. They are to be handled ever so carefully and gently. We would never allow our jewels to fall into the hands of someone who was careless or uncaring. We must find that safe place to plant our dreams until such time they are ready to bloom.

We should not be discouraged if the dream doesn't appear to be growing. As long as the seed has taken root, in due season, the harvest will come. It's no different than when we plant bulbs in the fall. During the winter, the ground is bare, cold and hard. At times, we may even forget about the bulb. Then one spring morning, we get a glimpse of what has been preparing to bloom all winter.

Personal – A dream is a mirror revealing your deepest self. It's the thing that we never have to state verbally, but the thing that we find ourselves constantly trying to create. Our dreams are a collection of the stuff that we bring to the party. They are who we are. They are the things that we try to run away from, and the things that we run to. It's the baggage that we get from others, and the baggage that we give to others. It's where we can be transparent and acknowledge our greatness, as well as our weaknesses. It's who we are.

Powerful – Dreams provide a powerful foundation in our pursuit of purpose and destiny.

It's what directs us to areas that seem so foreign, yet feel so right. It's the DNA of our core. We can't change the DNA; however, we can decide how it's used. It's what causes us to be driven and gives us passion. It allows us to be courageous in the face of fear and uncertainty. It allow us to leave the past, appreciate the present, and pursue the future

Protected – Dreams should be protected and shared with only those who are trustworthy. Many times our love ones, in their attempt to be supportive, will destroy our dreams. They think they know what is best for us. Their intentions are pure, but many times they have no idea of the number of dreams they have destroyed. Because we love them as much as they love us, we suffer silently, never letting them know the pain that they have caused.

There are also people who are envious, and really don't want us to achieve our dreams. Their intentions are not pure. These are the people that we have to exercise extreme caution with regarding to our dreams. They may be friends or family members. If we are not careful, we will begin to believe naysayers, doubters and haters. These negative thoughts will sprout as weeds that will only choke our dreams.

Why Aren't Dreams Fulfilled?

Many people make choices based on what others want, or what will be easiest. Most of us have an idea of what we feel would make us happy, productive and fulfilled. Yet, for whatever reason, we make a conscious decision to place our dreams on hold, and look for choices that will cause the least amount of discomfort.

We have been taught to live inside a box of what we think we can have and what we already know. We settle for what we have and give up our dreams. A friend of mine, who was unemployed at the time, was allowing her current circumstance to define her future. She stated that she would never own a house. I agreed with her. My response seemed to startle her. I very calmly replied that if she truly felt that way, then indeed she would never own a house. She took that conversation to heart, and recently closed on her new home.

The trend or movement in this direction is so overwhelming, that without some kind of structure for support, we get swept away. It becomes almost impossible for us to buck the tide and hold onto our vision alone. We forget what it is that we truly want, what brings us joy and fulfillment.

Beware of the Gremlins

The Gremlin attempts to maintain the status quo. When I start to dream and explore new possibilities, my Gremlins have a way of showing up. They say things like:

- "Who are you to want more out of life? How dare you!"

- "I don't have enough time, money, etc to realize my dreams."

- "I can't or I shouldn't.

We all have gremlins – it's important to be aware of our gremlins. These gremlins are often holding us back from having the life we want! The Gremlin doesn't like it when we start changing, or when we start moving out of our comfort zones and going for what we think we can have.

Ten Tips to Turn Your Dreams into Reality

1. Visualization – How will you know that you've achieved your dream? What will success look like? What will it feel like? If my dream is to take a vacation, at what point during the trip will I feel that I've realized my dream? Would it be arriving at my destination and checking into the hotel? It probably would be when I am able to turn the visuals in my mind into a reality. For example, lying next to the pool, with a cool drink, nice book, and friendly conversation.

2. Write Your Vision – Write your vision and keep it in plain sight throughout the journey. Once you write your vision, it becomes real. You are more focused on the really important things. You will find yourself meeting people who have similar interests. You will be presented with opportunities that were unavailable in the past. Don't take my word for this, try it.

3. Planning – Someone once said, if you don't know where you are going, any road will take you there. Good planning includes goals and objectives that are specific, measurable, attainable, reasonable, and time based.

4. Find a Coach – Everyone should have a coach, or someone who can help them achieve their goals. The coach provides accountability and encouragement in working toward a more balanced and fulfilled life. This relationship should be based on trust and complete confidentiality.

5. Self-Acknowledgement – It's important to make a list of successes and accomplishments that you've celebrated in the past, as well as your strengths. We spend so much time focusing on the negative, and not enough time acknowledging our successes and accomplishments. As we begin to view ourselves more positively, our self-esteem and self-worth will increase.

6. Name and Change Self-Defeating Attitudes – I believe it's important to deal with the following self-defeating attitudes:

Fear: Fear has a way of crippling us. If we are not careful, we will become prisoners to the thing that we fear. We must confront that thing that we fear in order to conquer it. If we are not able to confront our fears, then we will become slaves to that thing that we fear.

Negativity: Negativity is contagious. It's counterproductive and self-serving. Have you ever been in a great mood and found yourself in the company of a negative person? If you are not careful, your whole mood will change; you will feel as if life is being sucked from your body. The air in the room takes on a different feel. You begin to see the glass as half empty, versus half filled. We have to live our live so that our dreams can bloom in their due season, and not be killed by the weeds of negativity. This includes our own negativity.

Insecurities: It's funny how most people find it difficult to acknowledge their insecurities. If I admit that I am insecure, then

I must be weak. The sad thing is that we spend so much time trying to camouflage our insecurities, rather than confronting and changing them.

Understanding our Insecurities

Inner Need	If Missing, I Feel	Common Symptoms
Belonging	Insecure	Over-compensation Emotional lows and highs
Worth	Inferior	Competition, self-doubt Need for Validation
Competence	Inadequate	Comparison with Specific People
Purpose	Illegitimate	Compulsive and driven Spirit, defeat, depression

7. **Perseverance** – The journey in pursuit of our dreams requires us to persevere and remain focused. It's okay if we have to recreate our dreams from time to time. We are all a work in progress (WIP).

8. **Belief** – If you believe, you can dream. Half of the journey is believing in something or someone. When we believe, there is an expectation that something will happen. Believing activates our hope and faith.

9. **Courage** – Remain strong, even when you don't feel strong. It doesn't take much courage when the task at hand is easy. However,

when the obstacles are great and you feel all alone and fear is overtaking you, it takes courage to persevere.

10. Pray Often – We have to know that we are not alone. It is comforting to know that, when life's struggles are too much for us to bear, or we need direction, that we can ask for and receive divine help.

Follow your dreams, for as you dream, so shall you become. Imagine the possibilities and believe that you can do it.

Resources

Taming your Gremlins by Rick Carson

Leadership Conference at TSOD Church, Ratcliff KY

Notes:

ABOUT THE AUTHOR

Dr. Kanteasa Elanta Rowell

Dr. Rowell is President and CEO of **PATHS of Success, Inc**. She conducts workshops and seminars that have been presented throughout the United States and abroad. Dr. Rowell has been certified by the Professional Woman Network as a Save Our Youth and Diversity Trainer. She is certified and experienced in facilitating workshops and seminars on the following topics, but not limited to: Organizational Leadership, Educational Leadership, Team Building, Struggling Teens, Parenting, Youth Leadership, Success, and Cultural Diversity. Dr. Rowell has been recognized by the Manchester's Who's Who for Executive and Professional Women.

Dr. Rowell's knowledge and expertise in professionalism and leadership is supported by years of work experience with Orange County Publics Schools, School District of Hillsborough County, and Palm Beach County School System in both instructional and administrative roles. Dr. Rowell is also an adjunct professor with the University of Phoenix, Belhaven College, and Grand Canyon University.

Organizations
- Professional Woman Network
- American Association of University Women
- National Association of Female Executives
- Society for Human Resource Management
- National Association for the Advancement of Colored People
- Joy Zone – Youth Ministry
- College Liaison – College Awareness Teen Ministry
- Women's Ministry – Rejoice In The Lord Ministries
- Zeta Phi Beta Sorority, Inc.

Contact
PATHS of Success, Inc.
kanteasa@pathsofsuccess.org
(407) 358-8244

ELEVEN

PARENTING: ROLE-MODELING AND CARING FOR THE YOUTH

By Dr. Kanteasa Rowell

One of life's most rewarding experiences is parenting. Whether the child is a biological offspring, an adopted child, or a stepchild, the benefits remain the same. Youth receive guidance outside of the home by various individuals that they come into contact with on a regular basis: educators, mentors, spiritual advisors, law enforcement officers and others. Youth often look up to and imitate the lifestyles and personalities of these individuals. It is so important that we direct our children to the company of those who will provide positive role modeling, encourage them to participate in enrichment activities, and steer them away from illegal activities.

While many families rely on both parental incomes, and with the increasing number of single parent family households, youth today spends an enormous amount of time with other caretakers. Caretakers look after the youth both inside and outside of the youth's residences. Parents trust and rely on caretakers to provide a positive environment for youth during the times in which the parents are away. This chapter gives insights into parenting, role-modeling, providing structure, rewarding, and providing consequences for inappropriate behavior. The chapter concludes with various ways to bond with the youth and the most inexpensive gift – love.

Parenting

The parent's role in rearing is never complete. Responsibilities to and for our offspring never end; they adjust to accommodate the years of growth and maturity. From the first year of birth, nourishing the child with a bottle through the years of marriage, (and the possibility of being caretaker of the grandchildren), parenting continues on and on. The roles of parents vary from day-to-day. Each day of parenting ends with additional experiences and milestones. No other adult responsibility compares to being a parent. And let's face it, **parenting is a life-long career!**

Role Modeling

One important life-molding responsibility for a parent or caretaker is the task of setting a good example for their dependents. Many times a child imitates and often duplicates the actions they see performed. Respect, care, love, consideration, high self-esteem, and honesty are some of the many characteristics from which children thrive. Parents should model these positive behaviors independent of another's action. Modeling disrespectful, inappropriate actions can distort a young child's judgment of how they should react to certain situations. I use the term modeling due to the fact that, whenever a child is near, we (parents) are on center stage. **The behaviors that we perform when our children are present are the same behaviors that our children are likely to perform in our absence.** Ask yourself these questions:

Exercise

1. Are you honest in communication with friends and family? When was the last time you "fibbed" or told a "white lie"? List these here:

_____

_____

_____

2. Were your children aware of your dishonesty? How do you feel about telling your child to tell the truth, if you do not? Share your feelings.

_____

_____

_____

3. With whom are you dishonest? Can you begin to tell the truth with these people?

_____

_____

_____

4. In what ways are you a positive role model for your child?

_____

_____

_____

One of the most mind-boggling phrases that I heard while growing up was, "Do as I say, not as I do." I have no idea when that statement was coined, but I do know how I felt about it. I often wondered why a parent or caretaker behaved in ways (in front of me) that they did not want me to emulate. Not only did they allow me to witness behaviors they thought were inappropriate, these same caretakers then told me not to do the things that I had just witnessed! Do you think that was confusing? Similar to the phrase, "You are what you eat," the same applies, "You can't be what you can't see." It is very important for adults to model acts that they would be proud to see their youth performing. What messages are you sending to the youth by your actions? **Remember, when you watch the behavior of your children, often it is the mirror image of what they see in your behavior.** If you lie, you cannot (with any sense of credibility) tell your child not to lie; if you cheat (take a little extra of something and not pay for it), then how can you tell your child not to steal? Think about it carefully. Right or wrong, you are the role model for your child.

Structure

Rearing today's youth requires structure. Structure is required to steer youth in a positive direction. If youth are not reared in a structured environment and lifestyle, they tend to venture out more into less desirable locations (gangs, for example), and into less desirable situations (pre-marital sex, teenage pregnancies, tolerating abuse). Today's youth require structure in the form of a path that will lead them to success. Through a map that you and your child create, he or she is able to move towards a desired outcome. Your helping them create structure helps to create an atmosphere ripe for success.

Structured activities vary from household to household and by interests, faiths, religion, and so forth. Structured activities can take the form of a camping trip with the family to participating in organized sports, both competitive and non-competitive. Structured spiritual activities include church choir, praise groups, mime team, and music lessons. Dancing lessons and gymnastics, the debate team, cheerleading, sports, and academic bowl clubs are also structured. Another structured family event may be eating dinner together, and prayer before meals and bedtime.

As caretakers, we should closely monitor the activities that our children are involved in or observing. (Monitor the television, for example. While there are excellent educational programs, there are also highly violent shows, as well). Watch what your child is watching and listen to the music that they hear. YOU be the judge about what is appropriate or not.

Rewards

The topic of rewards tends to elicit mixed emotions. Some parents firmly believe that they owe their children nothing for behaving appropriately. There are others who reward their children for various things such as getting good grades in school, carrying out an extra chore, babysitting a sibling, and so forth. The reaction to rewarding children varies from one extreme to another.

Being a mother and having professional expertise in the field of education and business, I have witnessed the benefits of rewards. I firmly believe in rewarding an individual (including children) for a job well done. Rewards increase intended and wanted outcomes. A proven method of getting an individual to perform is to show the person gratitude and appreciation through either a tangible or intangible method.

Rewards come in many forms. Rewards aren't always tangible. A hug, a kiss, and a thank you, are all forms of rewards. Some rewards are seasonally specific, age appropriate and situational. Just as you wouldn't kiss your boss to show appreciation for the bonus that you earned, you wouldn't purchase a tie for your six year old for completing an extra chore. Rewards for youth may include permission to invite a friend to a dinner outing, purchasing a bicycle, hosting a party, giving gift cards, a toy item, a special trip, a sleepover with friends, a certificate, a free day from chores, and so many others. When deciding on a reward for your child, allow your mind to roam freely. Be creative when deciding on a reward. One important thing to remember is to stay within your budget. Don't over-spend and not be able to enjoy the reward with your child while trying to figure out how you will afford the bill. Discuss with co-workers, associates, and family members the success they have experienced from rewarding the youth. Remember that rewarding can be a wonderful experience for you and your child.

Consequences

Each action deserves a reaction. Sometimes the acts that our children perform are inappropriate (i.e. stealing, screaming, or temper tantrums in stores). Those inappropriate actions cause parents to become upset or embarrassed. Surely there are times when we are SO proud of our child, but there are numerous times when we want to hide underneath a rock in embarrassment! Importantly, we should not shelter our emotions from our children. It is perfectly fine for our youth to know how we feel about the decisions they make and the actions they perform. If we are upset, we must tell them.

On the other hand, it requires less thought and less negative emotions to applaud a good deed. People in general tend to have an array of items in a treasure bag to reward the good deeds our children perform. It is my sincere prayer that the rewards from treasure boxes are being depleted in response to good deeds performed by youth. It is important to praise our youths for appropriate behaviors and the good deeds they perform. I am so moved by youth and wish to see them engaged in positive activities.

Parents, teachers, and caretakers are thrilled to quickly take credit for appropriate actions performed by young people. As you would have imagined, we are just as quick to dismiss inappropriate behavior of our child ("He couldn't have done that!") or be in a state of denial. We would prefer to have someone (anyone other than ourselves) deal with the inappropriate actions. Reinforcing (or ignoring) a bad decision could turn devastating if repeated, depending upon the type (or lack of) action. Good practice is to design a behavior management system to increase wanted behaviors. Do you have consequences in place for inappropriate actions? **Consequences decrease unwanted behavior.** (By consequences, I am not referring to a beating or physically harming your child. Instead, I am suggesting age-appropriate consequences such as time-out for young children, and taking away privileges such as driving for the older youth.)

Simplifying Life With Your Children

Rearing a child can be simplified with an organized routine. Creating a daily schedule eliminates the stress of piecing tasks together from memory throughout the course of the day. A written blue print (to-do list) allows your child to follow tasks in an efficient manner. (I know that when I wake up in the morning and view my "to-do list", my day starts in a much more organized and less-stressed way.)

Simplify your life. By simplifying, you will be not only a good role model for your child regarding time management and prioritization, but you will find yourself being more calm if you have a step-by-step listing of "to-do's". By utilizing ten minutes before going to bed to write down and prioritize the tasks that are to be carried out the following day, it simplifies your "Tomorrow". (Yes, I am aware that the majority of our time is devoted to our professional career, and that is an additional reason why it is more important to plan ahead, so that we do not forget tasks and place additional stress upon ourselves.) Convenient tools that we use to simplify our days, weeks, and months include planners, desk calendars, electronic planning devices, cellular planning devices and organizers.

When planning for your "Tomorrow", be certain to include those easily forgettable minutes needed for transition. We often schedule tasks back-to-back. Be sure to include the time required to travel from one event with your child to the next. Generally, my son finishes soccer practice at 5:30pm, so I am careful not to schedule dinner preparation from 5:30 p.m. - 6:30 p.m. Unrealistic planning creates unrealistic expectation and unnecessary stress. (In such situations, thirty minutes of dinner preparation would be lost in the travel home, unless you live directly across the street from the soccer field!) Unrealistic planning has thrown my schedules off balance and placed me back to square one, leaving me cramming tasks in even after the "scheduled" bedtime. An unrealistic schedule has resulted in my having hectic days. Now that I plan my days realistically, I live a more simple life. What are some strategies that you can implement to live a more simple life? A SIMPLE LIFE IS CONTAGIOUS!

Bonding

TV Vocabulary

While viewing a weekly family show, compete with youth to both see and hear the names of the most items and/or words that begin with the first letter of the child's first or last name during the commercials only. You can also search for items that begin with the first or last letter of other family members' names. For example, if the child's name is Nathaniel, yell out the name of every item or word that begins with the letter "N". If the child's name is Brittainy, yell out every item or word that begins with the letter "B". Continue this pattern for the duration of the show. The individual who locates the most is the winner. The purpose for counting items during commercial time only is so that the family is able to enjoy the show itself. See the sample recording chart below.

Sample recording chart.

This chart was used for the family name Idlebird.

TV Vocabluary - Letter 'I'	
1. Ice cream	6. Indeed
2. Ice	7. Increase
3. Idol	8. Incline
4. Import	9. Incredible
5. Inside	10. Independent

Additional Adult/Youth Bonding Activities:	
Lunch in the park	Arts and crafts
Movie day/night	Car shows
Read books together	Circus
Prepare meals together	Theme parks
Mom/daughter day at the salon	Video games
Son/Father day at the barber	Bowling
Family day at the spa	Church events/outings
Family beach outing	Academic flashcards
Visit child at school for lunch	Road trips
Family shopping spree	Scheduled family TV time
Sporting events	Family exercise schedule
Clean the home together	Visit relatives
Camping trip	Finance/Budgeting lessons
Family cruises	Banking – deposits earned from completing chores
College visits	Performing arts and museums

A bonding activity does not have to be extravagant or expensive. The youth appreciates attention and quality time from their caretakers. My son continues to remind me that he doesn't care if I can afford to purchase expensive things for him. His action shows me that he prefers my time spent with him over my treasures spent on him. **Bonding soothes the soul!**

Love

The most precious, inexpensive gift that you can give a child is love. Children long to know that a parent or caretaker cares about their feelings and well being. Love increases self-esteem and decreases the need for a child to succumb to peer pressure.

I leave you with this poem:

> *Love is sweet;*
> *Love is kind.*
> *A daily dose*
> *I'm sure the youth wouldn't mind.*
> *Love is real;*
> *Love is strong.*
> *At times a roller coaster;*
> *But just hold on.*
> *Love is patient;*
> *Love is true.*
> *Love is from the heart;*
> *From ME to YOU.*
> — Dr. Kanteasa Rowell

Parenting is a precious gift from the heavenly Father. Role modeling allows us to guide and direct our children in positive directions. Structure allows individuals to steer the youth on a productive path. Rewards and consequences increase wanted behaviors, while decreasing unwanted behaviors. Simplification eliminates stress from the caretaker. Bonding activities bring the family members closer together. Love seals the package.

ABOUT THE AUTHOR

RIKI F. LOVEJOY-BLAYLOCK

Riki F. Lovejoy-Blaylock started receiving her own experience of working in a non-traditional environment when she entered the construction industry in 1985. Additionally, throughout her career, Riki has participated in college panel discussions and high school career days geared to encouraging women to choose non-traditional careers. Riki has been very active in the National Association of Women In Construction (NAWIC).

Riki has worked for major general contractors in the Orlando, Florida, market as a project manager and owned a carpentry subcontracting company in the early '90s. Additionally, she has worked on construction projects in Beijing, China and the Carribean. Currently Riki is the Executive Director for RFL Consulting Solutions, LLC, a construction management consulting firm with management contracts on projects throughout the country.

Riki is also the Executive Director for Breaking the Barriers, providing seminars and workshops that address diverse corporate cultures and non-traditional careers issues.

Riki has a B.S. in Business Management with a minor in Management Information Systems, is a certified Minority Business Enterprise through the Florida and Kentucky Minority Suppliers Development Council, as well as a certified Woman's Business Enterprise through the National Women Business Owners Corporation. In 2003–2004 Riki was named to Empire's *Who's Who of Business and Professional Executives*.

Contact
RFL Consulting Solutions, LLC
(407) 443-3423
rlovejoy@rfl-consulting.com
www.rfl-consulting.com
www.protrain.net

TWELVE

12 STEPS TO OVERCOMING THE SUPER WOMAN SYNDROME

By Riki Lovejoy

By now you have read about it, learned about it, talked about it, and perhaps have finally admitted to yourself that you are suffering from The Super Woman Syndrome. You may already have learned from experience what this Syndrome has done to you in terms of relationships, mental and emotional health, and most importantly, what it has done and/or will do to your physical health. The life you have created for yourself, your family, and your society, all came at the price of this Syndrome. You have now realized that suffering this Syndrome could ultimately end this life you have worked so hard to create. Have I scared you enough to stop the suffering? Are you ready for the cure?

Hopefully you are now asking yourself -- Is it an easy cure? Will this dreaded Syndrome take long to cure? Is the cure permanent? Let me be the first to tell you... there isn't a cure, but you may **overcome** this syndrome, and it will take a lifelong commitment to 'stay in remission' and remain free of the Syndrome. Overcoming is a multi-step, life changing process. It will be very difficult to stay focused on *Overcoming,* and you will lapse during the course of your "treatment". But if you have learned to love the person you are, and want to, at the very least, maintain the life you have, you will choose to participate in the "12-Steps to Overcoming the Super Woman Syndrome", starting today.

The 12-Step Overcoming process we will be outlining here is no mystery. Being the Superwomen that we are, we have already seen or heard about these steps in some fashion or another – a magazine article, another self-help book, a workshop at a woman's conference, even *The Oprah Winfrey Show*. We may have even practiced a couple of them – or maybe even all of them, at one time or another, but let's put it in some manner of order that we can now and forever remember . . . S T R E S S. Let's discuss and put into practice S T R E S S. Okay, now you truly believe I've lost it. Isn't the purpose of this chapter to overcome The Super Woman Syndrome, and therefore eliminate stress?!

It's simple...as a Super Woman, we seemingly cannot exist without stress, even though we will have a difficult time admitting this to ourselves; serious "withdrawals" could be more damaging than suffering through the Syndrome. So, look at S T R E S S as our "patch" to overcoming The Super Woman Syndrome, and its related stress. Let's see what S T R E S S is all about.

Survey and Strategize

First and foremost, you need a survey of what your life is about, as it exists today. This is not just writing down a list of the different roles you play in any given day, but this is about the honest, hard look within to admit you suffer from this Syndrome, and that you are ready and willing to Overcome. The survey is all about honoring yourself—your beauty, your intelligence and the fact that you are a unique individual that gets it done!

We have discovered that perfectionism is at the root of the Super Woman Syndrome. Webster's dictionary defines perfectionism as a *predilection for setting extremely high standards and being displeased with anything less.* So WE determine how things are supposed to be and strive to that end. "Oh well" or "Whatever" is not in a Super Woman's vocabulary.

I read a powerful statement not too long ago (author unknown), **We can choose how much and how long we suffer.** As a Super Woman, we expect TOTAL control, but this is control of our environment, our intimate society, maybe even our relationships. We lose TOTAL control when it comes to our self, our being – when it comes to me, me and me! We are under the delusion that, if our environment and relationships are under control in the manner which WE feel it must be – the perfect world – then me, myself and I will be perfectly content, happy… and not suffering through the Syndrome. Herein lies the addiction. As in any other "…aholic", admitting the problem is the very first step. So Step 1 - SURVEY within yourself.

The next step of the survey and strategizing (Step 2) is determining the various roles you play, admitting the time you spend for and with others. So what do we actually look at? I was going to create a great table or log for you to use which I personally felt would be PERFECT for you, but realized – Hey, I'm in this 12-step process myself (what a struggle!) and must let YOU use the method that is PERFECT FOR YOU! But I strongly encourage you to keep a journal using the following guideline, not just for the 'now' survey, but for reflection a year from now, five years from now, even ten years from now as you continue this journey. Watch how you improve and grow in the super strength of you.

Okay, here we grow....

1. Record on a weekly worksheet the time you go to bed and get up – the start and stop of your day. Be sure you include at least six to eight hours of sleep. You need the proper sleep to be at your best.

2. Indicate the hours you spend at work. We know already this takes the biggest chunk of your day. Later we will see how we can shave some of this time down to allow balance.

3. Schedule on your sheet two to three hours for each important person in your life today. This is not a daily requirement, but you need quality time with all the important people, not so much for them, but for you. These people are important to you for a reason – they are what make you whole.

4. Designate at least a half-hour of planning time weekly. You need to know where you are going each week so you can align your schedule efficiently.

5. Establish a ten-minute planning time daily for your TO DO list. Enjoy your first cup of coffee in the morning, reviewing what your day will be all about and how those last minute changes will fit in. Life is still going to happen – your schedule will need to be flexible to accommodate the changes. Believe it or not, you know this already and have already experienced and have become proficient in 'change management'. The difference here will be how you approach changes from here on out!

6. Designate a certain amount of time for chores and errands – DO NO MORE! Do a little every day instead of all on one day, i.e. clean the master bath on Monday, the guest bath on Tuesday, dust the bedrooms on Wednesday, and so on.

7. Give yourself two to three hours of time for professional personal care – facial, massage, life coach session, or exercise. You will find that clearing your mind on a regular basis provides for more efficiency in your everyday life. Much like the computer – every once in a while you have to turn it off because it has locked up.

8. Schedule time for fun and relaxation. See note 7 above!

9. Block out commuting time so you can see it in relation to your other plans. Include commuting for errands, taking Johnny to football and Suzie to ballet, and so forth. You will quickly see the double trips you are making.

10. Leave time open for doing absolutely nothing … totally unhurried. This will be your best "think" time.

*T*ake Control and Test (Steps 3 and 4)

Okay, you've completed the most honest, comprehensive survey of your life as it stands today. You've discovered, probably to your own amazement, just how much you really do for so many others and not for yourself. Next you have developed a strategy of handling it all by assigning specific time to your many roles. Remember, you should keep in mind that your 'assignments' should be flexible (you certainly don't want to add stress by having to clock-watch!) yet you need to be sure to include everything. Just because you are in this 12-Step Overcoming process, it doesn't mean everything that needs to be done or everyone else's needs will go away. And you most especially need to keep scheduling your personal time!

Taking control is all about gaining control of your precious time. Taking control is acknowledging…

- I CAN get control of my time.

- My time is valuable; it is just as valuable as everyone else's.

- I am not on call to everyone to do everything.

- I do not have to say 'yes' to all requests for my time.

- I do NOT have to be perfect at everything!

Another part to taking control is letting the people you serve know there are changes under way! Everyone is going to be affected in some manner with your Overcoming process, so you may as well put it out there at the get-go! As you acknowledge the value of your time, you will be learning some new phrases – "I would love to help you, but I am not able to do this for you at this moment", or "I would be happy to help you with this project, but I can only help on Mondays from 5:00 p.m. to 7:00 p.m." or the hardest of phrase for all of us Super Women – "No".

Here's where testing comes into play! Try out one of your newly learned statements by choosing an assignment or project that would be the least affected by your not 'being in charge'. Let's role play an example.

Mary: "Hi, Riki! As you know, I'm chairing the charity event for November 15th and I would love to have you co-chair with me."

Riki: (Knowing this means Mary and Riki will be doing all the work!) "Mary, I would love to assist with this event as it means a lot to me, too. However, I must tell you that with my current schedule, I will only be able to devote attention to the project on Mondays, between 5:00 and 7:00. Given all the details of the event, I strongly urge you to get more help, as you and I simply can't do it all!"

Mary: (Surprised but appreciative of your candor) "Well, thank you for your offer and at this point, any help is a lot of help! Now that you mention it, you're right; we will definitely need more help. I'll contact Suzie! See you next Monday!"

The following Monday, Riki leaves promptly at 7:00 to head for her next assignment – a relaxing, stress-free, hot bubble bath! In the end, the charity is quite successful as it was pulled off on time, within budget, and with some creative nuances that she came up with during those wonderful bubble bath sessions!

Edward M. Hallowell, M.D., author of *CrazyBusy: Overstretched, Overbooked, and About to Snap! Strategies for Coping in a World Gone ADD*, stated it so succinctly – "Play lies at the heart of creativity. Play can waste great quantities of time, in that it is not programmable to produce results on cue. Play goes off in tangents, knows no timetable, and can be subversive. But when play goes right, when the planets of the mind align, play transforms an old place into a new one." Taking control and testing opens the door to new places in your mind.

Relax and Resolve (Steps 5 and 6)

We're not talking about lying around doing not much of anything. No, here we are talking about relaxing your need for perfection. Have you ever thought about how 'the guys' get things done? Well let's consider these points…

OUR WAY	HIS WAY
• Bake cookies from scratch for the school party	• Has someone else do it, or buys at the grocery store
• Clean our own house from top to bottom, windows included	• Hires a housekeeper while out shooting a round of golf
• Responds personally to all calls, regardless of importance	• Determines nature of call; delegates calls of no importance
• Cooks dinners for everyone	• It's either cooked by you or he's eating out

Do you see the recurring theme on "his" way? Delegation, delegation, delegation. The guys know that perfection is impossible – getting it done is key. There are always individuals in our lives that can get it done. *Relax* your need for perfection and *resolve* to ask for help, delegate.

Enjoy and Enrich (Steps 7 and 8)

Are you enjoying your life that you have "Super Womaned" into? Remember we are talking honestly! I can assure you that if you actually said yes, you are lying to yourself. So ask the question again – are you enjoying your life today?

With our Overcoming process, enjoying life will be a reality. In fact, it is key to your Overcoming. Additionally, enriching your life with continued learning and discovery offers another level of enjoyment. Okay, you're now asking what is enjoying – what is enrichment?

Enjoying encompasses life at so many levels – remember that hot, bubble bath you had in your schedule? When was the last time you were with the girls giggling and guffawing your way through the evening? When was the last time you sat through a sunset or a sunrise? When was the last time you took an instructive class for one of your passions – cooking, dancing, stamp collecting? Enrichment and enjoyment feeds your creativity, lowers your blood pressure, lengthens your life span, keeps you young, and it is an essential part of the entire Process.

Streamline / Simplify (Steps 9 and 10)

One of the many new buzz words of the past couple of years is "to simplify." Streamlining processes, both personally and professionally, delegating, removing the "extras" from our lives, especially those that require attention from our already limited available schedule, are essential to these steps of your Overcoming process. You've heard it all before, some of it from childhood – don't drop your clothes on the floor – put it in the laundry or hang it up, close the drawers/doors you open, put things back where you got it, touch each piece of paper just once (taking care of it at the moment you see it), return calls in your personal "slow" time, throw away the junk mail without even opening! Little steps makes for giant leaps in your Overcoming process.

Suffer No More / Satisfaction (Steps 11 and 12)

We can choose how much and how long we suffer. By committing to our Overcoming process we've outlined here, you have chosen to end your suffering. You have strategized on the who and what and how; you have taken control and tested your strategy (and found it getting easier each time you said "No"), you've learned to relax your need for perfection and resolved to not be afraid to ask for help, you're learning or discovering something new on a more consistent and fun basis, and you have simplified your life to allow more time for yourself. If you have made it through the first 10 steps, you have reduced your stress and have "transform[ed] an old place into a new one" to become a more creative individual, and you have reached a level of satisfaction that hasn't been experienced probably since your childhood. Do you really not care about reaching this level of satisfaction? What do you have to lose if you don't follow S T R E S S? How long will it take for stress to take you from your life? *We can choose how much and how long we suffer.*

> *Someone will always be prettier.*
> *They will always be smarter.*
> *Their house will be bigger.*
> *They will drive a better car.*
> *Their children will do better in school.*
> *And their husband will fix more things around the house.*
> *So let it go,*

And love you and your circumstances.
Think about it.
The prettiest woman in the world can have hell in her heart.
And the most highly favored woman on your job may be unable to have
children.
And the richest woman you know,
She's got the car, the house; the clothes.... might be lonely.
And the word says if "I have not Love, I am nothing."
So, again, love you.
Love who you are.
Look in the mirror in the morning, smile and say,
"I am too blessed to be stressed and too anointed to be disappointed!"
"Winners make things happen.
Losers let things happen."
— Author Unknown

ABOUT THE AUTHOR

MYRTLE LOOBY

Myrtle Looby is the President and Primary Consultant of LEAP Training Consultants, based in Antigua and Barbuda. Having enjoyed a successful career as a trained educator of English and Communication Skills, she now makes keynote presentations, and designs and conducts outstanding workshops and training seminars throughout the Caribbean. Some of her most sought after workshops are on Customer Care, Communication Skills, Leadership, Effective Supervision, Team Building and Women's Issues.

Myrtle's background and expertise have contributed to the passion and dynamism that she brings to all aspects of her life, including community service. She is a founding member of the Professional Organization of Women in Antigua/Barbuda (P.O.W.A.), a member of the Advisory Committee of the Directorate of Gender Affairs in Antigua and Barbuda and a member of the Antigua Lions Club. As a Lion, she has held the position of Zone Chairperson, Region Chairperson, and District Trainer for District 60B. She is also an active member of her church community where she uses her expertise to conduct seminars with the Young Adults Group. Internationally, she serves on the Board of Advisors of The Professional Woman Network and is a member of the Professional Woman Speakers Bureau.

In fulfilling one of her lifelong dreams she has co-authored the recently published best-sellers, *Becoming the Professional Woman*, and *The Young Woman's Guide to Personal Success*. She is currently working on her sixth publication.

Myrtle holds a Bachelor of Arts in English and History, a Diploma in Education, a Certificate in Guidance Counseling and a Diploma in Gender and Development Studies.

Contact
LEAP Training Consultants
P.O. Box W704 Woods Centre
St. John's, Antigua
(268) 460-5504
guidance@candw.ag
www.prowomen.net

THIRTEEN

SISTERHOOD: THE NEED FOR ENCOURAGEMENT & SUPPORT

By Myrtle Looby

A wise woman once said, "Sisters are angels who lift us to our feet when our wings have trouble remembering how to fly." Like eagles, we can and do soar to great heights, but many of us believe that we can achieve and maintain the heights of success solely by the strength of our own wings! Yes, sisters can be angels who will support and lift us, but they can also be the wind beneath our wings, to propel us on. We have heard of many instances when women have done extraordinary things for the love of their female friends, from attending the Lamaze classes to being among the first to welcome the newborn. They are there at the diagnosis and remain constant before and after chemotherapy. They give us the "heads up" on the new vacancy that we should apply for and they take us out for dinner when we become the casualties of "downsizing." They attend our graduation many miles away and find the most intimate gifts for the bridal shower. These shared experiences enrich the lives of both the giver and the receiver, and enable them to be more supportive of others.

Yes, I can hear the response: "How can you say that when women are their own worst enemy?" That, my dear Sister, is one of the greatest myths that we have believed in for far too long.

"But, I have been hurt by women so many times," you say, "and now I do not know whom I can trust." Well, does the fact that we have been hurt by men mean that we should discount all that they are and have been in our life? Of course not! Then why should it be so for us women? We may also be guilty of expecting each woman friend to be the embodiment of the skills and abilities to satisfy our every need, whim and fancy, and when they don't, we deem the relationship a failure. In fact, when we acknowledge that each one has different strengths and areas that need to be improved, we become more empathetic and tend not to have unrealistic expectations of others.

"But women do not support other women," you say. "Can't you see how much friction there is among women in the workplace and even in our social lives?" I am afraid it does seem like that sometimes, but conflict is a part of life and you may be surprised to learn that we do not hold the monopoly for conflict in any sphere of life!

Can it be that we are too hard on ourselves and expect perfection in our relationships with other women, or is it that we spend a disproportionate amount of time nurturing our relationships with our men and children, and leave our female relationships to languish? Is it that we take our relationships with other women for granted and therefore do not value them for what they are worth?

"Do women really give each other encouragement and support?" Sure, we do, but there is always room for improvement. The more successful we become, the greater the challenges and the need for support. We still struggle with balancing the demands of work and home, and for some, we add Church, community work and studies. Oftentimes, the journey seems a lonely one, and we wish there was a listening ear, a supportive arm, or even a familiar form nearby to bolster our self-confidence.

Let's do this simple quiz. It's almost like looking at your reflection in a mirror and seeing yourself in a new light. Please check "Yes" or "No" in the appropriate column.

Have you ever......	Yes	No
1. Been a member of a women's group, network, or organization?		
2. Given or accepted advice from a woman?		
3. Mentored a woman in her career?		
4. Benefited from an article or book written by a woman or written an article or book for women?		
5. Received support from a woman when you were ill, sad or hurting?		
6. Needed to talk to a woman as only she would understand?		
7. Had a woman friend as a sounding board before making your decision?		
8. Had a woman as a role model, or been a role model for another woman?		

9. Said a prayer for another woman in need because of some personal crisis?		
10. Congratulated another woman on her success or that of someone close to her?		
11. Taken a woman for lunch or tea, or brought it in, when you thought she needed it most, or you were the woman in need?		
12. Gone on a "Girl's Night Out"?		
13. Allowed another woman to make a mistake and gain wisdom from it?		
14. Sat with a sister friend communicating with each other without saying a word, but each speaking from the heart?		
15. Spoken out in support of, or in defense of, another woman?		

If you checked "Yes" to most of these, and I am sure you did, then acknowledge that you, like other women, have been sharing love and support with others! Perhaps not as much as you would like, but the fact is, we generally devalue ourselves and our relationships with other females. We continue to define who we are by our relationships as wives, mothers and daughters, but not as friends. In addition, when we do, we allow others to determine the value of female relationships, and buy-in to the notion that they are mainly toxic. Here is the twist: It is when we devalue ourselves and subscribe to the myth that women are not supportive of their own kind that we become our "own worst enemy."

On the contrary, while it is in our relationships with both men and women that we develop as human beings, it is our relationships with women that help us to determine our authentic self. We look to other women and their experiences to model our behavior and to get guidelines that shape our life. Besides, no matter how accomplished or successful we are, no matter how much we love our men or how supportive our family is, no matter how much we think we are "keeping it all together," (as society tells us that we should), NO OTHER PERSON in the world can take the place of a "Sister friend."

Some sisters we have met and some we will never meet, but through all the years, from generation to generation, women have shared a common bond of sisterhood. We may call them "girlfriends," "sisters," "sister friends," or "woman friends," but we would not be who we are and where we have reached without their love and support. Besides, they are the antidote for the ailment that afflicts many of us in our struggle for success, when we fall into the trap of the Superwoman Syndrome. Experience has taught us that, when we mistakenly believe that we can "Have it all, Do it all, and Be it all," or when life throws hard punches at us and we are too weak to fight back, we can always rely on our sisterhood of friends to see us through. It is when we recognize and acknowledge our own value as women and the uniqueness of womanhood that we can begin to trust ourselves and others, and appreciate that we need one another for encouragement and support. No matter what the situation is, there is always a Sister to help us.

Sisterhood means different things for different people, but one thing is certain, they are like good undergarments. Selection is made with great care and often by trial and error, but when we do find a good brand and design, we become like partners for life - inseparable. Here are some characteristics we use to guide us when we make our selection:

- *Functionality.* Sister friends come into our lives for a season and a reason. We often outgrow them as our needs change. Just as different garments serve specific functions, so do our sister friends! Many women claim that they even need greater support as they get older.

- *Durability.* They should be able to weather the storms of life.

- *Support.* They should be prepared to give support when and where necessary, and keep us in good shape.

- *Confidentiality.* They are our trusted confidantes. In fact, they know us better than we know ourselves, and guard our secrets until we part.

- *Comfort and Compatibility.* We must feel comfortable in their company. There must be a good fit so that we can trust them with our secrets and vulnerabilities.

- *Dependability.* We can depend on them when the going gets rough for support or encouragement.

- *Availability.* This speaks for itself. They should be close enough but not too close, allowing space to "breathe."

- *Speaking Truth.* Although they keep our secrets, they should be honest enough to speak our truth so that we can make necessary life adjustments.

- *Life enhancing.* A Sister friend adds value to our life in some way. She engages us where we are, but leads us to a better place either by holding our hands, allowing us to climb on her back, or by pointing us to the way forward and helping us to avert danger. Like a good undergarment, she enhances our image as well as our self-esteem.

- *Needing special care.* Sisterhood denotes the sense of community, of trust and dependability, of support and encouragement, of empathy and caring, of a deep sense of knowing as only a woman would know. Sisterhood is sacred, but it needs nurturing and tender loving care for sustenance and survival.

My first lessons in Sisterhood were learned from my mother, as I grew up in my little village of Plymouth, Tobago, in the Caribbean. She was a friend, confidante, counselor, coach, baby sitter, and pillar of strength to many. Women from the village always came to her to discuss their domestic problems or complain about their over-demanding bosses. She was never too busy to lend an ear or give a word of advice. She cooked meals when they were ill, empathized with them when they were grieving, loaned money to tide them over difficult times, and even took care of their children for short periods when they had to be elsewhere. She had a sister friend who was a survivor of domestic violence. My mother taught her to make local delicacies so that she could regain her self-confidence and be financially independent. To this day, this woman is known for her homemade ice cream and souse (a soup-like meal made with salted meat, cucumbers and seasonings), and uses her income to take care of her grandchildren!

Many women in my village did their weekly laundry at the river. Oh, how they treasured those moments when they claimed their time and space, away from the eyes and ears of their men folk! And if they could, the rocks would echo the peals of laughter as the women shared their joys. The riverbanks would tell of tears that flowed with the heaves and sighs that punctuated sorrowful silences. Laundry day was an opportunity, in a safe and supportive environment, to bond with other women who could understand; who would sometimes assist them with their workload; who could feel their pain and share their joy, and from whom they gained the strength to carry them through another week. Our home remedies for aches and pains and children's ailments were prescribed and sometimes dispensed at the river!

As children frolicking in the shallow waters, we listened but did not always understand. What we learned, however, was that something special happened when women met and shared their stories. Some of my closest friends are women who grew up with me and had the river experience etched in their soul. We have developed an appreciation of the indomitable strength and sisterhood of women. We know that we need one another and still meet to share our stories, not at the river, but where ever and when ever we can.

Today, times have changed. We may not be able to meet our sisters in person for the weekly chat, but we are fortunate to have the Internet and the advanced technology that facilitates instant communication. Sisterhood now has a global dimension. Take for example, my friend Linda. We met as professionals years ago and, although we are separated by thousands of miles, we communicate by e-mail. She calls me "My Friend," and as only a woman would, she is able to read between the lines of my e-mails and realize that at times I am struggling with some challenges. A few months ago, we met again, and would have really liked to spend more time together, but that was not to be. However, on checking out of the hotel, I was handed a package that Linda had left at the front desk. It contained a motivational card and a refrigerator magnet which read, "Even on a cloudy day, the sun still shines." We had not spoken about my problems, yet Linda knew exactly what I needed for encouragement and support at that time. Her gesture was a like ray of sunlight, and I will always remember to look for the sunshine among the clouds. She is more than a friend. She is my Sister!"

Three friends, Patricia, Joan and Lucia, are members of their local professional women's organization that meets regularly for meetings and social events. The demands of their own businesses have kept them on different schedules, so they are rarely seen together. For the most part, they communicate by telephone and the Internet, and each fills a special void in the life of the others. Patricia, the motivator and prayer-warrior, is the sounding board for new business ideas and the counselor in personal crises. Joan and Lucia are the business and marketing experts who give advice and share their management and leadership skills. They treasure their friendship and the personal and professional gains that it brings through networking, and by sharing their wide range of experiences and insights.

Then there is Edwina, who is a member of the Big Brother Big Sister Organization. She has a penchant for mentoring young women as they enter the job market, or others embarking on a career change or needing to be their personal and professional best. She has opened her home to "Sisters" for their "Girls Night Out", or a respite after a hard week's work. Edwina is also wise enough to give you space to make mistakes, yet she is never too far to pick you up after the fall and soothe the pain.

Some sisters never say a word to us, but they "have our back." Some we may never meet, but having traveled that way before, they make sure that they leave a trail for us to follow, or red flags on those that we should not take. Maya Angelou is such a sister. Most of us have never met her, and chances are we may never meet, but when we read her books and listen to her reading her poetry or speaking to audiences, we can feel her hand clasped gently over ours as she leads the way, saying with her voice of woman wisdom, "Come, Sister, this way. No, not there," or, "Stand tall, Sister. They may never understand, but you are already enough!" Then we square our shoulders, hold our head high, take a quick inventory of our strengths, and press on.

Sister, the news is out. "Ms Have It All - Do It All - Be It All" is dead, or will soon die of self-inflicted wounds. She has already written her own obituary, which says that she had believed in the illusion of the "Self-sufficient woman", and was struck down by the ailment called the "Super Woman Syndrome." She was often disorganized, overworked, bitter and lonely. She had not trusted neither the wisdom nor the company of other women, so she lived like a caged bird, in self-limiting space, behind self-imposed walls. Her life has been unhappy and unfulfilled, and has been deprived of the support of her own kind, a choice she has lived to regret in her last days.

These are her words of advice for all women:

- You cannot do it all, nor can you do all, alone. When you expect perfection of your self, you demand it of others, and no one is perfect.

- Learn to trust yourself first so that you can trust others. Do not be afraid to let other women see your brokenness, because we are all vulnerable at some time. There are women waiting to help if you only open up and remove the walls around you. Just ask, and you shall receive.

- Be your authentic self. When others see that you are wearing the mask of the Super Woman, they may not come close. Remove the mask and let others see you for who you are. Then they will know exactly what you need.

- Be sincere. Life goes around in circles. You reap what you sow.

- Always look for the good in others, and make that person feel valued. Relationships are built by making others feel good about themselves.

- Sisterhood is reciprocal. If you need a Sister, be a Sister. Be a mentor, a coach, or a positive role model, and forge bonds with other women. We are all inter-connected.

- Some friends can respond better in crises than others. Recognize their limitations, and know on whom you can depend, and for what.

- Let your life add value to the lives of other women in some way. That's the least you can do.

- Make time for yourself and your Sisters, and nurture yourself and the relationships.

- Learn to listen. Sometimes all we need is a smile and a listening ear.

A Sisterhood Story

As if to bolster our faith in the importance of Sisterhood, someone sent me this story to share with others. I have seen different versions of it, but I have not been able to verify its authorship. As a fitting closure, I dedicate it to you and all the Sisters in your life.

To Sisters

A young wife sat on a sofa on a hot humid day drinking iced tea and visiting with her Mother. As they talked about life, about marriage, about the responsibilities of life, and the obligations of adulthood, the mother "clinked" the ice cubes in her glass thoughtfully, and turned a clear, sober glance upon her daughter.

"Don't forget your Sisters," she advised, swirling the tea leaves to the bottom of her glass. "They'll be more important as you get older. No matter how much you love your husband, no matter how much you love the children you may have, you are still going to need Sisters. Remember to go places with them now and then; do things with them. Remember that 'Sisters' means ALL the women... your girlfriends, your daughters, and all your other women relatives too. You'll need other women. Women always do."

"What a funny piece of advice!" the young woman thought. "Haven't I just gotten married? Haven't I just joined the couple-world? I'm now a married woman, for goodness sake! A grownup! Surely my husband and the family we may start will be all I need to make my life worthwhile!"

But she listened to her Mother. She kept contact with her Sisters, and made more women friends each year. As the years tumbled by, one after another, she gradually came to understand that her Mom really knew what she was talking about. As time and nature work their changes and their mysteries upon a woman, Sisters are the mainstays of her life.

After more than 50 years of living in this world, here is what I've learned:

Time passes.
Life happens.
Distance separates.
Children grow up.
Jobs come and go.
Love waxes and wanes.
Men don't do what they're supposed to do.
Hearts break.
Parents die.
Colleagues forget favors.
Careers end.
But.........

Sisters are there, no matter how much time and
how many miles are between you.
A girl friend is never farther away than needing her can reach.

When you have to walk that lonesome valley, and you have to walk it by yourself, the women in your life will be on the valley's rim, cheering you on, praying for you, pulling for you, intervening on your behalf, and waiting with open arms at the valley's end. Sometimes they will even break the rules and walk beside you, or come in and carry you out.

*Girlfriends, daughters, granddaughters, daughters-in-law, sisters,
sisters-in-law, mothers, grandmothers, aunties, nieces, cousins, and
extended family, all bless our life! The world wouldn't be the same
without women, and neither would I. When we began this adventure
called womanhood, we had no idea of the incredible joys
or sorrows that lay ahead.
Nor did we know how much we would need each other.
Every day we need each other still......*
— Author Unknown

Notes:

ABOUT THE AUTHOR

Pamela D. Burks

Pamela D. Burks, author, coach, trainer and respected business consultant has worked in Information Technology for Fortune 500 companies in Michigan and Georgia for over twenty years in various managerial, support and consultative positions. Her consulting firm, Burks Consulting Group, develops business structure, business and strategy planning and provides business coaching and training to entrepreneurs throughout the U.S.

As a certified coach specializing in the areas of Business and Personal Development, she works with business owners and professionals focused on growth and change helping others to take new actions and develop new ways to see their future while defeating personal and professional obstacles. She is a member of Coachville and a MasterMind member of Brilliance in Action coaching organizations.

Since 1984, she has trained professionals to expand their career opportunities using technology. She has expanded that training via the "Business Forum", a series of seminars and workshops, offered by Burks Consulting Group, and a joint venture, "Careers and Business" both designed to reach out and educate entrepreneurs.

As co-author of "*Self Esteem & Empowerment for Women*" and "*Overcoming the Super Woman Syndrome*", her writing aligns with her desire to help others achieve their goals and aspire to be better than the circumstances that surround them.

She is a member of the Coleman Research Group, Gerson Lehrman Group Council of Advisors, Dekalb County Chamber of Commerce, Professional Woman Speakers Bureau and other organizations devoted to excellence. She is on the Board of Directors of the Professional Woman Network and Xyon Integrated Solutions and also owns **Computer Skills Institute,** a computer skills training company. Burks Consulting Group is certified as a Woman Business Enterprise.

Contact
Burks Consulting Group
3653F Flakes Mill Rd #116
Decatur, GA 30034
404 312 1368
Pamela.Burks@BurksGroup.net
www.BurksConsulting.net

FOURTEEN

TAKING PERSONAL INVENTORY OF SUCCESS AND JOYS

By Pamela Burks

Your everyday successes are the smaller steps you make toward achieving a greater you. They can be as simple as the activities you completed when there were not enough hours in the day to get them done, but you did them anyway, or when you were **afraid** to try and "did it anyway". (For example: Reaching out to someone who might not have been very receptive to you, but you reached out anyway, and they may not have appreciated you, but…. it really was not about them, it was about you and what **you** accomplished.) These are the smaller accomplishments/successes so easily overlooked, but that combine to create the much bigger successes in your life. These are the small successes that you never hear about when the lives of successful people are discussed.

For instance, Madame C. J. Walker had to step out and sell that very first jar of scalp conditioner. I imagine she was scared (but did it anyway), especially during the year 1890! By overcoming that fear and achieving that small success, she became the first African-American woman self-made millionaire. Mary Kay, widowed with small children and no work related skills, overcame her fear and sold child psychology books door to door. As a result of her efforts, she became the founder of one of the largest cosmetic product firms in the United States. If either of these women did not acknowledge the smaller successes, they could not have been able to motivate themselves during the more difficult times to reach the bigger successes. And if these women that we regard so highly could acknowledge **their** smaller successes, surely we can do the same. So wake up ladies and smell the coffee! We need to walk the pathways of success that have been blazed for us, and acknowledge our own successes, just as others did.

One good way to capture "golden" moments of success so you can track your successful journey is to keep a journal. Oh, I can hear the groaning already. "I kept a diary as a little girl. That's kid stuff." Well, think again, Missy! This is the grown up version. Your journal is about your life **now**! Yes, you can include goals, hopes, dreams (and I encourage you to dream because dreams are the developing stages of goals yet to be accomplished), but in this journal, you will record your own "pat on the back", things that made you smile or laugh, acknowledgements by you or others of "a job well done" and what you did that "saved the day". There are those of us who don't have a "cheer team" to recognize us when we've done well, so we need to do it for ourselves. We **deserve** the praise and besides, who else could do a better job of recognizing us than ourselves! We are usually the acknowledgers of our family members, church groups, and even our work group's accomplishments! We know how to make people feel good about themselves. We need to do the same for ourselves. "Woo Hoo!" "Alright!" "You did it girl!" "I'm proud of you!" "I'm impressed!" See, we know what to say. We need to say it to ourselves… and mean it! Sometimes we don't realize just how valuable an effort we put forth, so the success and acknowledgment of it goes unnoticed. That's where the journal comes in. At the end of the day, even if you are lying in the bed about to close you eyes to end your day…jot a couple of notes in the journal. Did you run all the errands that needed to be completed, even though there was not enough time to do them all? Jot that down. Did you take dinner to a senior citizen, even though you were tired? Jot that down. Did you get the report/work completed by the deadline, even though you were given more work to do two hours before the deadline? Jot that down! You are the MA'AM, Ma'am! YOU made things happen today so that everything or everyone is prepared for tomorrow. Woo, Hoo! Congrats!! You had some every day successes, and I'm proud of you!

Now I know there are some folks that say, "That's just doing what you need to do to get through the day. That's not a success." Phooey! If you had not gotten it done, who else was going to get it done? No one! Discounting a success just because it's not a big success does not make it any less of a success. You can, however, feel unaccomplished and non-valued if you ignore or devalue your successes. "Celebrate, Celebrate, dance to the music!" and ignore the sourpuss who says, "It's not that big of a deal." Well, if it wasn't that big of a deal, why did they take the time to say anything at all? Remember, everybody's got an opinion, but all opinions are NOT valuable! Mary Kay learned how to sell door to door, and that small success led to developing and selling her own products. Know anybody with a pink Cadillac? I do! Her small success led to not only a big success for herself, but for women all around the world! "Celebrate, Celebrate, dance to the music!"

How do you celebrate? What about a once a month reward program? You can design your own reward programs, and the best part is, you can decide on all the available rewards to choose from. Treat yourself to a new dress or pair of shoes. (I love buying shoes!) If money is tight this month, treat yourself to your favorite dessert or bake a cake…. and eat it! You can have your cake and eat it too! Send the kids visiting for a weekend, and have the house to yourself for some much needed quiet time, or an opportunity to go out and stay up late doing something other than laundry (smile). You know what you like…. go for it! The successes are inside you, and you create them everyday. It's time we acknowledge them!

Make a list of the things with which you would like to be rewarded, and give each a ranking with #1 as the highest level. The #1 item is the item that you give yourself for the completion of your most challenging or most courageous task of the week or month. You decide when to reward yourself for this success and choose the #1 item. I suggest you reward yourself at the very least once a month.

Well, I feel better! Everybody needs to know they are successful, and sometimes that knowledge alone can make you feel better, even giddy! I personally vowed to remain a "Toys R Us" kid forever! I want to laugh, play, and have joy in the morning. Yes, joy! Its funny, a friend of mine asked me why I laugh so often. I joking said, "I feel happy, oh so happy!" mimicking the song. But later, when I thought about it, I really DO feel happy, not because I have everything I want, but because I enJOY the fun things. I can laugh at myself as easily as I can laugh with others. Joy is the emotion of happiness, delight and pleasure. For me, having joy and happiness is more of a conscious decision than the delivery of a "thing" that makes me happy. If I have to wait for something or someone else to make me happy, I could have a long wait between those happy feelings. So instead I choose to enJOY the things that ARE my life.

For example, I love dogs, and I always had a dog. But now, with my current busy schedule, I just can't have one, because I'd be out of town so much that the dog would rarely see me, and that's not a good life for the dog. My neighbor however, has the most darling black lab. When I watch him playing in the yard, it just makes me smile and sometimes laugh out loud. I'll tell you a quick story: I live in Atlanta, GA and we rarely get snow or ice, but the first year of the puppy's life we had an overnight ice storm, and in the morning the ground was covered with ice. Well, if you know anything about dogs, you know they are particular about walking on "new surfaces". The puppy saw the ice for the first time and was not amused, to say the least, but it was his response that was absolutely hilarious! He proceeded to try to break the ice in the driveway so that we could walk on the concrete by pouncing on it... then he tried to dig it up! Poor thing, he had no idea that if he just waited an hour, it would melt anyway. I got his antics on tape, and everyone who saw it laughed until they cried! We enJOYed that moment, and shared it with others so they could enJOY it with us. One of our other neighbors asked me a couple of days later, "Did you see that stupid dog try to dig up the ice... dumb dog!" They missed the enJOYment because they were too busy "being a grownup" and couldn't see the FUNny situation as funny!

Folks, we must learn how to lighten up, and live! Stress is the cause of major illnesses in this country, and the cure starts with deciding what's important enough to worry about, and accepting the other stuff as "rocks in the road". We need to keep rolling without stopping to pick up every rock in the road. You'll get jostled a little, but it shouldn't stop you. While talking about a work situation with a co-worker one day, he commented about the situation by saying, "It is what it is, so let's just move on." I've never forgotten that phrase, and will always appreciate him for teaching it to me. It is what it is! Stop trying to fix what you cannot fix. Stop worrying about what you cannot change. Does the Serenity Prayer come to mind for any of you? http://www.cptryon. org/prayer/special/serenity.html. Make a change where you have the ability to change, and the things that you cannot change? "It is what it is." Then, be prepared to make the next move when the opportunity presents itself (notice I said "be prepared"). Ok, I'm off my soapbox. We as individuals must realized that we can't fix everything, and every thing does not require our undivided attention. Go to the pet shop or the local humane society and play with a puppy. You'll end up laughing and feel better. I guarantee it!

Now that you know what makes me smile, what makes you smile? What gives you "joy"?

What do you currently recognize as joy in your life? What are your expectations of joy in your life? Have you allowed others to define joy and success for you? Oooh, you probably need to think about those questions. Take your time. I've got a few minutes. Hey, why don't you write the answers in your journal? Don't worry, you don't need anything fancy. For now use any avail paper in the room, but the next time you're out and about running errands, stop by a discount store and pick up a notebook. Some of the stores have actual journals, but if they don't, just pick up a plain spiral notebook. That'll do. So what did you come up with for answers?

Since we are not talking face to face, I'll share my answers with you. When I was younger and "building my career", my success was defined by employment status and annual income. When I was a part of the group, I wanted to be group lead. When I was group lead, I wanted to be supervisor, when I was supervisor I wanted to be a manger. But when I became a manager.... Whoa! I wanted my life back! For each position I move up to, there was a price to pay in time spent at the job, increasing amounts of work to complete, and responsibility for the productivity of others. Now, "I" had to redefine exactly how far up that ladder I was "willing" to go, based on what I was willing to give up. Next, was the money. Success was making your age in thousands of dollars. At age thirty-four, I wanted to make $34,000, and each year I wanted to keep up or surpass my age in annual income. I don't know where I got that silly idea, but I had it and I based **my** success meter on it. Nothing made me happy, and I wasn't interested in anything that was not in direct pursuit of that goal. Can you image how much control over my happiness I had given up just because I allowed an outside factor to determine my success! Well, guess what? I wasn't the only one with silly ideas. My cousin was very close to her paternal grandmother, and sought her grandmother's acknowledgement of her accomplishments and success before she would consider them successes for herself. If grandma didn't think much of her success, she wouldn't either. Grandma was motivated by finances, and only acknowledged successes that were revenue generating. And as a result, my cousin dismissed quite a number of community awards and accomplishments as unimportant events in her life. She missed the opportunity to enJOY her accomplishments. If you ask my cousin about her accomplishments, she would tell you she has not really accomplished much in her life. That's sad because after thirty years she still holds the track and field record for her high school and has been recognized by the state with a humanitarian award for community service.

So, how do YOU define your success? Your definition can have a major impact on what you acknowledge as joy. Everybody wants some success in their lives, but defining **your** success by another person's standards could result in missing the JOY of the accomplishment. Here is another journal question. What's important to you? Go ahead, make the list. I know, these are not easy questions, but at least try. What's important to me is completing something I started that was a little difficult to do. I enJOY the sense of accomplishing a task that was a little challenging. When I accomplish it, I celebrate and enJOY the moment. If you have children in your life, watch what they do when they achieve a goal… they celebrate everything, and we help them! When they dress themselves in the morning and get all the buttons buttoned correctly, we all do the "happy dance" and they enJOY the moment. But that same parent who does the "happy dance" when buttons are buttoned correctly, will not even buy a celebratory ice cream cone when she completes her online college course, while working a full time job and raising a child. "Celebrate! Celebrate! Dance to the music!" It's time to do the "happy dance"! We adults get so "caught up" seeking the next goal that we miss the one we just accomplished! If nothing else, jot down a "pat your self on the back" acknowledgement in your journal! Why? Because when the journal is full, you're going to schedule two hours out of your day to go back to the beginning of the journal and re-read every word. You know what you'll find? A personal account of all your accomplishments, frustrations, successes, and it'll be time to do the big "happy dance"! All the smaller successes will add up at the end of the journal, and the bigger successes, the progress you made, will be revealed.

All you Super Women out there fulfilling the roles of mother, sister, daughter caregiver, employee, friend, lover, guidance counselor, confidant, motivator, etc. not to mention the secondary roles you play, need to take a moment to just be YOU and acknowledge and inventory the successes of your life. If you have not kept a journal in the past, I strongly encourage you to start one. At first you may not know what to write in your journal. See the outline below to help you get started. But for right now, jot down what you completed in the last 3 months. Not just accomplishments for which you received awards, but simply what you completed. I'm guessing you'll be surprised at what you've done. I hope you look at your list, ~~and~~ feel good, and take pleasure in seeing your successes on paper. I hope you feel….. joy in realizing you are a mover and a shaker in your world.

> *"I hope you still feel small when you stand beside the ocean.*
> *Whenever one door closes I hope one more opens.*
> *Promise me that you'll give faith a fighting chance.*
> *And if you get the choice to sit it out or dance…I hope you dance. "*
> — Lee Ann Womack

Helpful journaling hints: http://www.uoregon.edu/~counsel/journal.htm

Suggested Journaling Outline

Write answers to the 5 questions below at the end of each day until you are comfortable with "free form" of your journal entries:

- What have I completed today?

_____

_____

_____

- What did I do above and beyond what I planned to do today?

_____

_____

_____

- What made me laugh today?

_____

_____

_____

- What made me cry today?

_____

_____

_____

- What did I do that I'm proud of today?

_____

_____

_____

God Bless,
Pamela Burks

Notes:

ABOUT THE AUTHOR

ELIZABETH PALM

This chapter is dedicated to my children Angela, Tina, and George with love. They are my inspiration, my encouragement, and a tremendous source of happiness. They have seen and experienced the effects and results of the superwoman syndrome; and no one laughs harder than we do when the cape reveals its truths.

Elizabeth Palm, President of Palm Consulting Group, is a Certified Professional Consultant located in Southeast Michigan. Ms. Palm has a degree in Business Management and is certified in Human Resources. Her expertise includes corporate training, human resource support, and business management. Ms. Palm is an active member of The Professional Woman Network and serves as a senior member on the PWN International Advisory Board.

Ms. Palm is highly knowledgeable on issues regarding customer service, human resources, diversity, self-improvement, women's issues and professionalism. Ms. Palm has conducted training in both formal and informal settings nationwide for thousands of corporate employees including executive management teams. Ms. Palm has a passion for sharing knowledge and guiding others on their journey toward success. Her presentations are interesting, insightful, and thought provoking. She is also a co-author of *Customer Service & Professionalism for Women* and *The Young Woman's Guide for Personal Success* available in the PWN library.

Ms. Palm is available as a keynote speaker and seminar leader for groups, organizations or associations both locally and nationally.

Contact
Palm Consulting Group
PMB 343
19186 Fort St.
Riverview, MI 48193
(734) 282-8442
www.protrain.net

FIFTEEN

CREATING A CALM & PEACEFUL LIFE

By Elizabeth M. Palm

Calm and peaceful; it sounds like a location deep in the forest. Or maybe it describes an illusionary time and place. When you think about these two words, it might be helpful to remember that they represent a moment in time, or perhaps a state of being.

So why is it we want or expect either of these conditions to last a whole day? It would be great if you could stop what seems like total chaos in your day, wouldn't it? We live in a world where information comes to us at the speed of light, people enter and exit our lives constantly, and we are expected to be happy, no matter what happens. We *are* the superwomen of the world.

With every experience, our lives are moving right and left, while our emotions are bouncing up and down. We live in a catch everything, do everything, and don't- miss- a -thing society. Are your thoughts racing after reading that sentence? Did you feel rushed, or did you recognize something familiar happening in your life?

Perhaps the suggestion of creating a calm and peaceful life might seem a bit of a stretch for you. For some women, not "doing it all" is the most absurd thought of the day. Many women find it downright impossible to delegate or let go of the reins long enough to enjoy a quiet moment. Does that description fit you? You know it is not impossible, it does however, take a little practice and effort. Does this mean moments of chaos, adversity, or disagreements will disappear? I'm sure you will agree that this is not likely, and probably unrealistic to think it might happen. It is, however, time to realize you can find *some* balance in your life through recognition of patterns in your thoughts and actions, or knowing your options and limits. Once you do, you will also realize you can create a calm and peaceful life for yourself.

Check & Balance

In every profession there is a routine check and balance that identifies problem areas, or distinguishes what does and does not work well. You can apply this principle or practice by conducting your own check and balance. Of course, there will always be things that show up at the most inconvenient time to throw you off balance. One of my favorite experiences came during a self-improvement course; the instructor spoke of a seemingly familiar, yet hectic day in which a series of unexpected events occurred. At the end of the day she said she had repeated the same response to each situation: she threw her hands open and said with a smile, "Well, this is pretty inconvenient." While we all chuckled for a moment, it became clear that it helps to accept the fact that life provides us with inconvenient moments (Check). How you react or respond to these little inconvenient moments makes all the difference (Balance). Could you smile when things get a little crazy? It might be worth a try. Do you see what I mean? This is not rocket science; it's common sense with a dash of humor mixed in.

Just for fun, let's see how crazy things really are, shall we? You can start by answering a few yes or no questions. These are easy and probably familiar; don't hesitate in your answer, just jot down your first response:

• I'm feeling overwhelmed on a regular basis. _____

• I'm always tired or feel low on energy. _____

• It's so hard to say "no" when others ask me to do something. _____

• My daily routine can be classified as insane. _____

• I've considered giving myself "time-outs" just to slow down. _____

• I am overwhelmed at my level of commitment to others. _____

• I'm distracted easily and can't remember anything lately. _____

It should come as no surprise to see more yes answers than no. You might be asking yourself, "Why is it always so chaotic, and how do I stop the madness enough to calm things down?" Remember that chaos is a moment in time. Maybe it's not chaos; maybe what you're experiencing is a lack of organization. There are many great benefits to be had by adding some level of organization and structure in our lives.

I would encourage you to think about where you are today. Call it a mini-self evaluation. Take a moment to consider your health, medications you may take, and how often you really exercise. Think about the last time you did something for *you*, or gave yourself a time-out. Now ask yourself some better questions:

- If I don't change some of my 'yes' answers to 'no', where will I end up?

- What will my health be like in two or five years if I don't make any changes?

- What is the worst that can happen if I include a few calm and peaceful moments in my life today?

These are your checkpoints. Do you sense a balance in your life, or would you agree it might be time for a change? It takes constant effort to balance the activity in our lives. So when the scale tips a little too far, you do something different. Take action, go beyond *thinking* something must change and put the energy behind the motion. You know there are some life events that you cannot control or avoid; it is not necessary to define them here. However, for everything else there are actions you can take to bring those chaotic moments back into balance.

Chaos is Over-Rated

It bears repeating that you cannot eliminate chaos from your life; however, you can reduce the intensity by eliminating some of the factors that create chaos. As one friend in the medical business put it, "Root out the cause and stop chasing the symptoms." Ask a mother or teacher what they do to bring calm into the room. Either of these individuals can provide great, yet simple examples of actions that put chaos in its place. A favorite illustration occurs in the classroom. Just before class begins, all the students are talking. There are multiple conversations going on at once. You've been there and experienced the chaos of loud talking, high-pitched laughter, and so on, right? One teacher has to gain all the students attention at once, so she simply flips the light switch a few times. Attention is drawn to the front of the room and quiet erupts. It's a marvelous thing; no screaming over the noise, just a flip of the switch. This is not limited to classrooms. Meeting facilitators and seminar leaders use music or video clips to entertain the participants as they enter the room. When the music goes down or the lights come up, the attention is shifted to the front of the room. Imagine yourself listening to the quiet sounds of your house for a few minutes. You can find ways to calm things down at work too; be creative with professionalism! *Chaos is overrated*; you can create your own calm moments by applying these few examples at home or work.

Calm in 15 Minutes

Creating calm can be as simple as turning down the volume on life's activities for 15 minutes a day. Observe any particular day in your life:

- How much noise and distraction can you identify?

- How much is external, such as television, radio, traffic, or other people?

- How much of it is internal? (This is usually your inner voice telling you to worry, or reminding you of the ten other things you need to do today.)

- What are some ways you can quiet or slow down your inner voice?

- How much of this external and internal noise or distraction can you reduce or eliminate?

You can make a huge difference with 15 minutes a day. Since you're in charge, you can take these 15 minutes anywhere, anytime, anyway you want. Morning, noon or evening, you pick. Realize and experience yourself in control by taking 15 minutes to reduce your stress level, clear your mind, focus your thoughts and breathe. You will be amazed at how different you will feel at the end of the day.

Here are a few ideas you can use to incorporate 15 minutes of calm in your day. I encourage you to use one, if not all:

- **Take a Walk** – Whether you are at work or at home. There is always a break in the action to allow you to step away, walk around the block, around the building, and focus only on your breathing.

- **Meditate** – Take a few minutes to quiet those worries and fears. Think of meditation as purposeful thinking. Concentrate on your breathing or gaze out a window and watch the trees, watch how easily they move back and forth when the wind blows.

- **Slow Down** – Instead of driving on the freeway the full way home, pick a safe route and drive through the neighborhood for a few blocks. The speed limit is much slower. Notice how much quieter and less hectic it can be.

- **Exercise** – All exercise is not fast paced, does not have to occur in a gym, or cost a large sum of money. Do a few simple stretches, and focus on each movement as you gently pull and flex the muscles.

- **Write it Down** – When chaos gets the best of you, take a few minutes to write your thoughts and feeling down on paper. Save it or shred it, it makes all the difference in the world to just get it out of your head and release the emotions.

- **Make a List** – Make a list of all the things you have to do today. Write the task then give it a priority number (1-Must be done, 2-Needs to be done sometime today, 3-This can wait for another day). There are many other ways you can calm life down. You are the creator, the artist, the one in charge. Make it happen, make it a part of your routine. You can start with five minutes and work up to 15 minutes if you must. The key is to take action. Build your momentum 15 minutes at a time.

Options and Limits

Creating peaceful times in your life may require you to set some personal limits. Ask a friend to help, if this is hard to do on your own. Do you really need to have more, or is there enough in your life? Are you trying to 'keep up' with the social standards created by someone else? It is very important to make sure you are not creating problems for yourself by trying to do things that don't fit your lifestyle. By taking a few minutes to clear your head and calm things down, you'll be surprised at what you accomplish. If you just stop and give yourself time to think, you will most certainly identify your options and your limitations. Some women create their own chaos by exceeding their limits or forgetting they have options. Do you know what your limits and options are? What can you do differently? It takes practice (and a few helpful words) to get started and on your way. The secret is to use your own words. Here are a few ideas to get you started; write in some thoughts or responses you can feel comfortable with:

- Are you feeling overwhelmed? List some ways you can delegate or ask for help.

  "I could really use a hand completing this project. Can you help?"

  _____

  _____

  _____

- Is it hard for you to say 'no'? Then set a limit on the number of times you say yes.

  "I'm already committed to help ___; I wouldn't want to over-commit my time."

  _____

  _____

  _____

- List a few of your current commitments.

  "Schedule time on your calendar for yourself."

  _____

  _____

  _____

You always have two choices. Those two choices are how you set your limits and know your options. It may sound like this: yes or no, right or left, stop or go; it applies to everything. Every situation creates two options. You can choose to live with the hectic pace, or create a few peaceful moments. It is ultimately your choice. Others will respect and appreciate you more if you work within your limits and options.

It is not necessary to provide a list of excuses or reasons why you are not available. You know it is more stressful if you try to talk your way out of something, instead of working within your limits or identifying your options. How does that work? Simple statements or responses work the best. Here are a few ways you can say no, bow out gracefully, or use when you are overwhelmed:

- "That doesn't work for me. Is there another way I can help (sets your limits)?"

- "Thanks for thinking of me, but my schedule is full; can we do it another time?"

- "I'm not available. Have you asked _____ or tried _____ (offer ideas or options)?"

Once you know how to set your own limits, you can help others know their options. This creates a great ripple effect, and you will help others at the same time. It is difficult for women to say no because we were raised to be helpful and accommodating. You can still be helpful and say no. These are just a few ideas. Practice or rehearse in the mirror, and get familiar with the tone of voice you will use. Say it with a smile. It helps to get a sense of the freedom the word no gives you, as well.

Ok, sometimes we just can't say no. If you feel you must do something, then offer some suggestions or ideas that worked for you before you commit your time. When the situation compels you to say yes, then be specific on your availability. The key is to find a statement or response that you can be comfortable with when you say it. Here are some ideas to get you thinking in that direction:

- "I can help for an hour on Saturday. Does that work for you?"

- "This week is bad for me; I can help you next week on Tuesday evening?"

- "Did you try this solution? I found it really helped me."

Now write a few statements or responses in your own words:

- _____

- _____

- _____

- _____

Of course when you can help, it is good to be available. However, as women we tend to over-commit, which often puts our own personal needs on the back burner, and those needs go unfulfilled. Or worse, we suffer burnout and call it 'stress'. Being all things to all people is just not possible. The best thing to do is be true to yourself. Sometimes the kindest thing you can do is say 'no'. The key to knowing when to stop yourself is when you experience the slightest bit of hesitation, or you feel your body suddenly get tense. You know when to do it, but you just need to know it's ok and perfectly acceptable to say no sometimes. If all else fails, take a few minutes to think about your answer, or check your calendar before you commit to anything beyond offering helpful suggestions.

Finding Balance

Finding balance in our lives can be like eating an elephant, you can only take one bite at a time, and it takes a while to finish! Balancing family, friends, and a career can be time consuming and a cause of great stress in our lives. What happens when you try to balance all this? You become tired, frustrated, and irritable. In reality, making everyone happy is just an impossible task. Have you tried it? Did it result in more turmoil and headache than you could ever imagine? Of course it did. Have you ever thought, "It would be great to have world peace. It would be even better if I could just have a little peace right here in my own little corner of the world." We must have some sense of balance.

Let's put it in perspective:

• Describe four scenarios that are chaotic in your life today.

_____

_____

_____

- Now, using five words or less for each scenario above, what can you do to calm things down or make it work better?

_____

_____

_____

- Think of a scale – one side is weighed down with frustration and over commitment. What are some "actions" you can take to balance the scale?

Tracking your commitments and efforts will help you realize how easy it is to add some calm and peaceful moments into your schedule. Use a planner or pocket calendar to jot down what you have scheduled. There will be a few times when you can't write another task or errand in the little box! That is your signal to stop. You absolutely must write in time for yourself. Try this: 15 minutes in the morning, another 15 while dinner is cooking (or being delivered), and 15 more before bed. There, you now have 45 minutes to just collect your thoughts, or write down some solutions or actions you can take. How about writing down all the things you accomplished or resolved today? Now there is something you can feel good about!

Now, go back and look at your answers to the questions, as they will reveal some insight or enlightenment you didn't notice before. Do you see any familiar patterns? Maybe you can recognize some repeated thoughts or actions that you could change to bring some calm or peace into your life.

Need more help? There are many great presentations and seminars out there offering insight and ideas on how to balance your life. Of the many I have attended, I have found that each one offers a level of enlightenment that I can use to balance the scales in my life. I encourage you to find one or two that you can attend.

Creating a calm and peaceful life is a never-ending endeavor; make it fun, enlightening, and tap into the many sources of support available to you. There are plenty of stars in the sky, take a quiet moment to enjoy them. I wish you a multitude of calm and peaceful moments!

Book References

There Must Be More Than This by Judith Wright

The Power of Focus for Women by Fran Hewitt/Les Hewitt

The Little Book of Letting Go by Hugh Prather

How to Stop Worrying and Start Living by Dale Carnegie

ABOUT THE AUTHOR

Sunni Boehme, MSP

"Oh, boy! More Joy!" are Life Success Coach Sunni Boehme's favorite words. Sunni has helped thousands of women find more joy and fulfillment in their careers, relationships, and other important areas of their lives. With a Master's degree in Spiritual Psychology, she has dedicated her life to overcoming the major life issues that impact women everywhere in today's fast-paced world. Sunni is the author of *Mirror, Mirror... True Stories of Manifestation to Inspire the Magic Within You,* spinning delightful and captivating tales of overcoming fears and making her dreams reality while traveling throughout Europe and the Middle East.

Her book "Mirror,Mirror".....true stories of adventures and manifestation to inspire the magic within you. She wrote it to help women to conquer their fears and learn to trust that they can manifest a life to fulfill their dreams.

She was an award-winning Mary Kay Director until 1983 when a major car accident changed everything about her life. A Reiki Master since 1981 she has been teaching manifestation, healing and metaphysics in business and relationships for over 36 years. Ms. Boehme is a member of the National Speakers Assoc. of Wisconsin, Women's Information Network, Women Business Owner's Network, The Breakfast Club Network, and The Professional Woman Network. Her energizing and dynamic programs offer women the wisdom she has garnered as a teacher, business owner, speaker, and world traveler. She has been teaching the "Laws of Attraction" for over 30 years and is best known for her workshops on "How to Get What You Want NOW" and the Women's self esteem building workshops "Awaken the Goddess Within You".

Contact
Global Goddess Enterprises
PO Box 070125
Milwaukee, WI 53207
(414) 482-8971
sunniboehme@hotmail.com
www.sunniboehme.com

SIXTEEN

RESOLVING CONFLICT WITH GRACE AND EASE

By Sunni Boehme

Resolve conflict with grace and ease? You are probably thinking that even these words are "in conflict" with one another. Read on!

American society glorifies triumphing over conflict. This is evident in the movies and TV shows we watch, the news we read and hear, and even the language we use. Every problem becomes a fight. We fight cavities and cancer, declare war on wrinkles, drugs and poverty, and congratulate the winners and survivors. We have forgotten there is a graceful way to get what we want. Resolving conflicts with grace and ease is a wonderful skill to learn, and a wonderful way to live.

There will always be conflicts in our lives because the energy that shakes things up always stimulates growth, or at least provides the opportunity for growth if we choose to look at conflict in this fashion. Conflict is not a bad thing. In fact, it is possible to learn how to recognize the opportunities contained in conflict and use them to accelerate our growth…more on that later.

The big problem is when the EGO has to win. We invest so much time and energy building our "stories" about how we have been wronged, or how we are right, that the solution gets lost in the squabble. Attachment to who is "right" is often the cause of why it takes so long to discover the real source of the conflict or challenge. Let me give you an example.

Jen's Story

Jen's mom, Mary, was my client and was beginning to see wonderful coaching results in her own life. One day, Mary asked me if I would see her 22-year-old daughter, Jen, because she was so worried about her. Jen was drinking too much and blamed it on her job, which she hated so much that she dreaded going into work each day. She worked in a cramped space with desks that faced each other and lacked privacy panels. Gena, the woman who sat at the desk across from Jen's, swore constantly and raged on and on about people she hated and the rotten things that were happening in her life. Jen just wanted to work and be left alone, but Gena was always distracting her.

Jen had no peace in her life. She barely made enough to pay her bills, and was constantly afraid she would lose her job. Her self-esteem was so low that she felt trapped and continued to allow Gena's abusive behavior to impact her. Jen had started to self-medicate by drinking too much, so she was often hung-over in the morning, which caused even more misery. She was too afraid to say anything to her boss, because he was new and uncertain about his new management position. He had been an accountant in the firm and because of seniority, had sort of fallen into the management position and felt very insecure.

During our first coaching session, Jen sobbed through the first 45 minutes, in between spurts of her current reality. Luckily, her mom had filled me in on much of what was going on. Jen was so attached to replaying the victim scenario that she couldn't let go of that outcome. I finally stopped her. I had to derail her from feeling that there was no hope. It was the first time I had ever suggested this course of action to a client. I had read about these things and tried them in my own life, but this time she needed a miracle, so I pulled out all the stops and took the risk.

"Jen, you need a miracle!" I said.

She sobbed.

"Getting you out of this rut could take months of traditional therapy, but right now and right here, I am going to give you something that can help you. Are you willing to do something really daring?" I asked.

She sobbed and nodded yes.

"I understand this is a really difficult situation, and it feels hopeless right now, so would you be willing to try something and then call me each day and tell me the results?"

She looked at me and stopped crying. (Whew) Slowly, hesitantly, she said, "Yes."

So I began. "At the moment you dread going into work.... is that true?"

"Yes," she replied.

"Well, I don't blame you. I would, too. I don't like swearing either, and I like to work in peace and quiet. So how would you like to learn some new ways to create a bubble of peace and quiet around you?" I asked.

Now she was intrigued and giggled a little… like she thought I might be nuts. I had to completely fracture her frequency of FEAR. She was being consumed by her fear, which was getting worse each day, and actually attracting more abuse from Gena.

"Do you know that the color blue is very healing and creates peace and calm?" I asked.

"Yes," she said.

"When you drive into work each morning, what do you think about?"

She shared with me a scenario of fear and dread, just waiting for Gena to attack. I stopped her because she could have gone on and on, but at least she wasn't sobbing any more.

I asked her, "What if you could have a completely different experience tomorrow in the office?"

Now she did look at me like I was nuts. I had to completely engage her in being willing to see that she could possibly have a different outcome.

I told her the following:

1. I want you to think about blue lights and blue water and blue sky when you go to sleep tonight, so that you get a good, restful night's sleep (without drinking any alcohol so that it would be just natural sleep).

2. Tomorrow morning, when you are driving into work, I want you to think about walking into the office surrounded with blue light… calm and peaceful. (This thought would focus her mind on peaceful thoughts, instead of the usual fearful ones she engaged on her drive to work.)

3. When you walk into the office, I want you to see every light in the office as a blue light and feel that the blue light is flooding the office with peaceful energy.

She giggled...she was beginning to have an emotional experience and have fun with it. I continued:

4. When you look at Gena, even when she is talking at you, simply think "There is only love between us." Keep thinking that, no matter what she says. Just send love. It will keep you in a peaceful place and she will probably stop ranting, because she won't be getting the kind of reaction she usually gets from you. Every time you think of her, just think, "There is only Love between us." You will be creating a powerful healing force.

5. Then, for the next five days, call me to tell me of your experiences that day.

She agreed. I wrote the five steps down for her. Then I sent her off on her assignment for "solution."

I could hardly wait to hear her results. During the day, I kept sending her positive thoughts and reinforcement. That first day, she called me at exactly 5:30, as soon as she got home. She was giddy with excitement and feeling powerful, because she saw that her good thoughts had shifted the whole day. She said she had enjoyed a great night's sleep, and her drive to work had been more peaceful than she could ever remember. When she walked into work she felt powerful, because she was thinking that the blue light would be shining healing energy on everyone. Gena didn't even come to work that day, so she had a full day to experience some peace, and play with her new energy. She discovered that she had a purpose. She could be the "blue light, healing fairy", and she laughed. I was so excited for her, encouraged her, and praised her.

The second day she was happy and shocked because Gena hadn't bothered her all day, but more importantly, hadn't spewed any negative curses at her. Jen was gaining confidence and seeing results. I challenged her to find ways to compliment people the next day.

At 5:30 on the third day, my phone rang. Jen had such exciting results. She had so much fun thinking of positive things to say to people, which helped raise the energy throughout the office. She felt like she was making a difference everywhere. Gena stayed away from her again, and she had a peaceful and productive day. I told her that the reason Gena acted so hateful is that she probably came from a really hate-filled home life, and she didn't know any different way of behaving. I told Jen how lucky she was that she came from a home with such loving, understanding, and supportive parents, and that she was truly blessed. Now she was focusing her energies on positives, receiving positive results, and getting happier.

On the fourth day, Jen offered to help the new boss with a special project, even complimenting him for taking on the tough management job. She had offered him some support and she felt good about it. Gena stayed at her desk more that day, and they chatted a bit. None of the angry energy displayed.

The fifth day brought a most amazing surprise. Jen actually called me early in the afternoon, because something so astonishing had happened. Jen had been taking walks at lunchtime to avoid the negative noon gossip, which really helped her to get a break and breathe some fresh air. When she got back from her walk, on her desk in a Styrofoam cup was one single rose. A note said, "You are the best friend I have ever had."...... from Gena. Jen cried when she told me, and so did I. The blessing had worked so quickly and deeply.

Within a month, Jen called me to report that her new boss had given her a raise and a promotion as his personal assistant, which included a different office situation. She stopped depending upon alcohol, and had a much more positive outlook on life.

The blessing of "There is only love between us" really works in every situation. I have used it hundreds of times myself, and have taught it to thousands of clients. It simply resolves everything "in grace and ease" for the good of all.

Over my twenty years of being a Life Coach, most of my new clients have come to me because they are miserable in their relationships, be it marriage or job or money. They are experiencing conflicts at every level, even with themselves. Yes, you have a relationship with your job; when you spend more time hating it than enjoying it, there's a conflict. Yes, you have a relationship with money; if you're spending more than you earn, there's a conflict. You create conflict within yourself because of not honoring boundaries. All of these relationships will, at some time, need conflict resolution. Why not resolve them with grace and ease?

A New Way to Understand Conflict

Years ago, I studied *A Course in Miracles*. One of the lessons was "Nothing is ever as it seems." I began to look beyond the way things seemed to be, to get out of my "pity party," and find peace and contentment. I first had to find those within myself, and then within my surroundings. I learned to ask myself questions like, "How can I love my job today?" and "What do I love about my life today?" and was amazed at the positive changes that occurred in my life.

Gerald Jambolsky wrote a powerful book that opened worlds for me called *Love is Letting Go of Fear*. His premise is that when people are in fear, there is conflict. Hmmmm. We need to start asking, "How can we make this environment safe so that people will talk with each other and want to resolve conflicts …. with grace and ease?"

The words of Marianne Williamson, author of *A Woman's Worth*, really expanded the concept of empowerment through profound thoughts like, "There is only Love between us," which Jen had so successfully applied in her work situation.

… with Grace and Ease—those words can make all the difference. When we focus our energy and attention on the conflict, it grows. When we shift our attention to "How can we gracefully and easily find a solution?", the energy begins to flow toward a solution that works for all involved.

Helping Others Resolve Conflict with Grace and Ease

The Superwoman usually takes on any conflict that occurs in her environment and tries to find a solution by herself. She lets each side vent, totally convinced that she can solve this, whatever "this" is. In doing so, she often becomes a punching bag, because the people around her are letting all the stories of "he said, she said" escalate, with Superwoman caught in the middle. It takes a terrible emotional toll on her, and when she tries and tries and tries to find solutions, often others will not let it be resolved. She is frustrated, brings it home with her, drags it around with her, and queries her friends or colleagues about possible solutions. Whatever the conflict is, it becomes a much larger problem, and involves many more people than it ever needs to.

When a person comes to you with a complaint….. listen for a short time… maybe five minutes. If you let them go on for much longer, he or she is just using you to build the story, the anger, and add energy to the conflict.

The first question to ask is, "Do you want to see this resolved?" The most usual reaction to this first question is, "Well, of course I do!"

The next question, the powerful question you ask is, "How can this be resolved with grace and ease?" Then be quiet and listen.

If the person or people start complaining again, stop the flow immediately. Say in a calm voice, "I gave you time to tell me what the problem is. You told me you wanted to see this resolved, so now I am asking you (again), how do you see that this could be resolved with grace and ease?"

At first, there will probably be some confusion, for this is a whole new way of facing a problem and looking for a solution. It would be a rare person who has already thought of some constructive solution ideas. Ask the parties to write down their ideas for a graceful and easy solution. Encourage their willingness to look for a solution, explaining to them that this is a great opportunity for them to learn some new skills in finding graceful and easy solutions. Give a time frame for them to come back to you with a range of solutions.

By handling it in this way,

1. They will feel heard.

2. They will feel encouraged to look for new ways, and that you will be willing to listen to them.

3. The process of finding solutions with grace and ease has already been set into motion, and the emotional battering that has been going on will immediately begin to shift.

Resolving Conflict with Grace and Ease in Our Own Lives - Take Action

When you have a situation in your life that needs healing (conflict resolution / graceful solution), here are the steps you can use to help yourself.

1. Take a look at the problem (without your emotional attachment).

2. Ask for divine guidance to see a graceful and easy solution for the good of all.

3. Release your need to make the other person or situation look bad…. "There is only love between us, and we both want a graceful and easy solution."

4. Know that love heals everything.

5. Believe in miracles.

6. "There is only love between us." Keep saying it, no matter what.

By using these words whenever conflict arises in your life, whether that conflict is with people, situations, or within yourself, you will soon be handling every situation you encounter with grace and ease.

EXERCISE: Resolving Relationship Issues with Grace and Ease

If you have a friend, co-worker, or relative who has been a continuing source of frustration, anguish or anger, ask yourself the following questions. Begin by writing the person's name at the top of a sheet of paper. If you have a photo of that person, place it along side the name. Working quickly, write down your answers to the following questions:

1. What is the aspect of him/her that I absolutely can't stand?

2. What is the dominant feeling I associate with him/her?

3. What did he/she do that I absolutely can't forgive?

4. What feelings does he/she trigger in me?

(Keep it simple: fear, anger, sadness)

Now, go through the following sentence completions that relate to the person. Repeat each of these as many times as you can, filling in the blank with a different response each time:

1. I am angry that _____

2. I am sad that _____

3. I am scared that _____

(Write all of these, noticing the feelings that come up in your body as you write.)

Now that you have some basic information about your relationship with this person, go into a more advanced area.

1. Assume for a moment that we invite people into our lives to help us learn a lesson that we could not learn any other way. What did you need to learn from him/her?

2. What need did this person meet in your life when you first encountered him/her?

(This need could be something you are not proud of.)

3. What need is he/she still meeting in your life?

4. Ask if you are willing to release this person from playing this painful role in your life. In other words, are you willing to learn the lessons you have been learning from him/her in some other way?

5. Are you willing to forgive yourself and him/her for bringing each other so much pain?

Recommended Reading

After writing this article, I started reading *The New Agreements in the Workplace: Releasing the Human Spirit,* by David Dibble. It is a great support and plan to implement these exact concepts in the workplace, and how David, as a Consultant to major corporations, has been shifting energy in the most amazing ways.

A Woman's Worth by Marianne Williamson

Love is Letting Go of Fear by Gerold Jambolsky

The Secret by Rhonda Byrne

ABOUT THE AUTHOR

SHARYN YONKMAN

Sharyn Lynn Yonkman is the founder and principal consultant for Lynn Consulting Group, a personal and professional development training organization. Lynn Consulting specializes in career advancement skills for the professional woman, helping her in achieving personal excellence. As a passionate advocate of women's self-empowerment and life balance issues, Sharyn offers special expertise in dealing with transition and change in the workplace, as well as programs designed for those of the baby-boomer generation.

As former CFO of several high-profile retail and hospitality companies, Ms. Yonkman has gained valuable in-depth financial and managerial experience in the corporate community providing the knowledge for cost-effective solutions for today's business challenges. A sampling of the training programs available includes: Sensitivity and Diversity, Professional Image, Power of the Positive, Professional Customer Service, Self-empowerment, Assertiveness, Handling Conflict and Emotions, Women-Wellness Work, and Getting Over Getting Older. Additionally, customized curriculum is available to meet your specific business needs. One-on-one individual executive personal coaching is also available.

Born, raised, and educated in New Jersey, Sharyn moved to southern California a decade ago. This bi-coastal experience provides her a unique perspective to be able to incorporate the best of each coast's business culture and convey that knowledge to her clients.

Ms. Yonkman is a co-author of Remarkable Women, an anthology project with Jennifer O'Neil, Dottie Walters, and Marci Shimoff. Additionally, she is currently completing an upcoming solo project for baby-boomer women facing the challenges of moving from the first act of life to the second. Trainer, motivational speaker, author, and coach, Ms. Yonkman is available internationally to help the individual or organization with professional developmental needs.

Contact
Lynn Consulting Group
P.O. Box 1266
Ventura, CA 93002
(805) 677-3117
Lynnconsult@yahoo.net
www.protrain.net

SEVENTEEN

YOUR QUIET PLACE

By Sharyn L. Yonkman

"A quiet mind cureth all."
— Robert Burton, English Clergyman 1577-1640

The definition of "quiet" is: motionless, without noise, undisturbed. Stillness (v) to make or become calm.

When it comes to dealing with the demands of the world that are stretching you to your limits, I am not sure that a quiet mind is the cure all, but I am certain it is a wonderful place to start.

Many women wait for that far off mystical day when the world will magically stop, and there will be time for them. They do not realize that they deserve some time alone to be quiet, without justifying it by multi-tasking. Relaxation is essential to maintain optimum mental and physical health. It is in your best interests, as well as those close to you, that you take care of yourself and your own needs.

Taking time to be quiet may seem like a luxury you can ill afford, but I must tell you that you cannot afford not to take the time to be quiet. Alone time is about working on the most important relationship you will ever have— the one with yourself.

When was the last time you took the time to just be with you?

Most women would protest that the biggest obstacle keeping them from nurturing themselves is finding the time. So here is where we must get creative, think outside the box, and look for ways to give you a little free time, even a few hours a week. Small increments of time scattered throughout the week can help you maintain more personal power.

Here are a few examples to help you start thinking of ways to create free time.

- Delegate at the office – REALLY!

- Check into baby-sitting coops.

- Send out the laundry.

- Rotate responsibility for children, so you have a few evenings or weekends off.

- Do "Take Out" for dinner.

- Take a break from your partner. Time off, even an evening off to be alone, helps.

- Get outside help with housework.

Now, write down at least three ways that fit your personal circumstances. List the ways that you will find the time to be quiet. Also, determine how you might handle possible infringements on that time.

1. _____

2. _____

3. _____

4. _____

I challenge you to begin your journey within now, by reading on and doing the exercises that follow. I must warn you, if you do not go within, you will most certainly go without.

Fighting the SWS with the Three S's

Silence, Solitude, and **Sanctuary** is my Rx for you in your battle against feeling overwhelmed. Let us look at each of these, and explore ways to incorporate these soothing balms into your life.

The First "S" - Silence

"Love silence, even in the mind… True silence is the rest of the mind, and is to the spirit what sleep is to the body—nourishment and refreshment."
— William Penn

Silence forces you back into your inner world, and draws upon your own inner resources. Often our modern day 'too-busy syndrome' is a subconscious way to keep us from our deeper feelings. We stay so busy that we cannot possibly have the time to look inside. Quiet time, by its nature, is reflective. Do not be afraid of it. Rather, see it as an exciting opportunity to learn more about the unique being that you are.

What might you discover in reflective silence that is frightening?

_____

_____

_____

What might you discover in reflective silence that is truly amazing?

_____

_____

_____

Take a SILENCE break. Make a pledge to nurture yourself by taking at least ten minutes a day to connect with the peace and tranquility of silence.

Below are some steps you can take to facilitate your silence break:

- Walk in the woods

- Go outdoors and listen to the sounds of nature

If you cannot get outdoors:

- Turn off machines -- TV, radio, computer, telephone, answering machine, etc.

- Remove yourself from the sound of any repetitive noise, such as a ticking clock

If you cannot find time for silence during the day, wait for everyone to go to sleep, or wake up a few minutes early for your ten minutes of silence.

Make a list of things you will do to insure your quiet time, keeping in mind the above suggestions, and adding others specific to your environment:

1. _____

2. _____

3. _____

4. _____

"Silence is golden." This saying survives, for it is a truism. What golden treasures will you mine in your quiet mind?

The Second "S" - <u>Solitude</u>

Solitude is actually a presence and not an absence. It is the presence of you exploring and developing an inner life.

Solitude can be a state of mind and, therefore, found anywhere, anytime. This state of mind allows you to just be with yourself, rather than always be in relationships with others. It offers you the space to listen to yourself.

Why Solitude? To be creative, you must have time away from distractions. This time allows you to concentrate and reflect, to think through ideas. To create.

Exercise

Make a list below of projects, ideas, concepts, challenges that need and deserve "alone" time.

1. _____

2. _____

3. _____

4. _____

A parting thought on solitude… Here is a quick and easy escape to solitude, even in a crowd. Keep a book on hand for any moment when you want to escape. Reading can take you away into a world of solitude, or relaxation, or an exotic adventure.

The Third "S" - <u>Sanctuary</u>

Sanctuaries typically are places of refuge, safe havens. This can be a rather elusive concept, but sanctuary really starts with a state of mind, which can be thought of as your sanctuary within.

The Sanctuary Within

There is a very special place inside us all where we can feel safe and find peace. Take some time to think about what that perfect place is for you. It can be anywhere—the mountains, the ocean, forest or desert. Anywhere. Create a place in your mind where you feel safe and happy. This is your special place. It's a place where you can go to find your personal truths and answers.

Exercise

Take the time now, while it is fresh in your mind, to locate your sanctuary within and write it down in the space below. Use adjectives to make it resonate with your inner self.

1. _____

2. _____

3. _____

4. _____

Sanctuary can also be found by being outdoors in nature, or by creating physical places for reflection. It is not the size of the space, but the quality of the mood it provides that matters.

Since every mood will not fit the same escape, choose the sanctuary de jour. Have a few in mind for your retreat. Below are some suggestions for creating your own sanctuary. (It does not have to be an entire room, just a small section—even a corner will do.) Next to each, jot down what mood that particular refuge will serve. Please list additional ones that are relevant to your specific situation in the blanks provided.

_____	Libraries / studies
_____	Big comfortable chairs
_____	A crackling fire
_____	Good reading lamps
_____	Window seats / reading nooks
_____	A greenhouse in your kitchen window
_____	A cozy chair at a window or on a porch
_____	
_____	
_____	

Many of us are creating special places to bathe by building luxury bathrooms. A therapeutic bath has the power to heal and soothe tension, and is pure bliss. The tub is also a good place to practice self-massages—a technique I discuss later in this chapter.

Here are some tips to create your bathing sanctuary, no matter how humble it may be:

- Take a warm bath, not hot, 95° to 100° (35C to 38C).

- Fill tub completely.

- Light candles and perhaps incense.

- Add aromatic oils to enhance your bathing experience.

- Choose scents such as bergamot, cedar wood, chamomile, lavender, or rose.

You can find a place of sanctuary by connecting with nature, whether you are inside or outside. Watching the birds or the leaves of the trees (especially in wind, rain or snow) outside your window is a connect with nature, as well as merely taking the time to water your plants and tending to their needs.

Consider growing herbs on your windowsill, or building a terrarium when you cannot get outdoors. You can connect with nature and solitude by building a Zen garden. Of course you could purchase one, but I suggest that the experience of building one will better help you to connect with nature, and find that elusive sanctuary within.

How to Build a Zen Garden

- Collect small stones and shells of various sizes, shapes and colors.

- Find a flat box, perhaps an old gift box, and partially fill it with sand. Use different colors and textures of sand.

- You can form the sand into interesting patterns with a small rake made out of a twig.

- Add your stones and shells any way that speaks to you.

- During your times of solitude, you can change the design and rake the sand to connect with nature.

Beyond the Three S's

Silence, solitude and sanctuary are terrific ways to get you on the road to finding your quiet place. Read on to discover more helpful healing tools, and make a commitment to employ some, if not all, of these techniques.

Meditation

> *"The secret of meditation is to become conscious*
> *of each moment of your existence."*
> — Thich Nhat Hahn

There are many forms of meditation, so I suggest you experiment with different forms until you find what works for you by using prerecorded meditations that are available in abundance. Do not be intimidated by the choices or fearful that you will not "do it correctly." Mediation is not all about the method, but is all about self-awareness. Basically, the purpose is to capture the present moment and enter the world within.

Exercise

Sitting comfortably cross legged or lying down, close your eyes and focus your attention on your breath. Drop into stillness, and be attentive to each breath. Breathe in calm and exhale anxiety.

When thoughts enter your mind, gently pull your awareness back to your breathing. If anything is distracting you, let it go. Focus on the moment and on the breath. Try and work up to at least 10 minutes, and then slowly bring your awareness back to the room.

Exercise

List below what steps you will take to find the type of mediation that works for you, and how and when you will learn to employ it:

1. _____

2. _____

3. _____

4. _____

Progressive Relaxation

Below is an excellent exercise to use as a prelude to any mediation practice:

Seated in a comfortable chair, with feet planted squarely on the floor, and arms resting on thighs, close your eyes and take several slow deep breaths. Bring your attention to your feet. Inhale deeply, tensing the feet. Then exhale and let the feet relax. Move up and use the same technique on your calves. Now bring your attention to your thighs and buttocks. Inhale and contract your buttock, pelvic muscles, and thighs. Then exhale and release. Now, your arms. Inhale and tense your arms. Exhale and release. Next, inhale and bring the shoulder blades together in back. Squeeze them together tightly, then exhale and release. Next, inhale and bring both shoulders up to your ears. Exhale and release, letting them drop toward the floor. Lastly, inhale and tighten the facial muscles, including the jaw. Exhale and release the tension, letting your jaw drop open. With your eyes still closed, slowly take several deep, relaxing breaths.

Self-Hypnosis

There is nothing supernatural about self-hypnosis. It is merely a state of focused concentration that can lead to inner communication. Your focus inward makes you less aware of your surroundings, and may allow you a sense of letting go.

We often enter and leave trance-like states without knowing it. Have you ever wondered where the time went while you where driving, or the hours at your computer, so engrossed that you lost the awareness of things around you? We all can relate to waiting at a red light, and suddenly hearing the horn of the car behind us because the light is now green.

You can experience trance in many situations. Here are some ways:

• Daydreaming	• Rocking
• Watching television	• Reading a book
• Running	• Dancing
• Listening to music	• Driving

Exercise

Try listening your way into a self-hypnotic trance (Note: Audio recordings are the simplest and most economical way to sample various guided imagery.)

- Make yourself comfortable.
- Sit quietly and concentrate intently on some word, sound or your breath.
- Visualize a pleasant scene and breathe in deeply relaxing body and mind.
- Focus your attention on the sound and scene, releasing all tension.
- Relax thoroughly, letting your thoughts drift.
- When ready, bring yourself slowly out of the trance.
- Remain still until you are totally alert and ready to move about.

Self-Massage

As the term implies, the only thing needed for self-massage is you. There is a natural reflex response in all of us to relieve discomfort through touch. Remember, as in most modalities, the more relaxed you remain, the greater the benefits you will receive from this practice.

Ear Massage

This exercise can be done almost anywhere and anytime.

- Using one hand on each side, stimulate the earlobes with your thumb and index finger.

- Pinch, then slowly pull - stretching the ear outward.

- Work your way from the lobe up and around the entire edge of the ear.

- Vigorously massage both your ears simultaneously until they feel warm, almost as if they were glowing.

Take Action

Now that we have discussed some very specific remedies to combat when you are feeling overwhelmed, as well as the means by which to find your quiet place, let us look at a random and varied list of things that may recharge and rejuvenate you. These can be anything from sensory pleasures to physical activity.

_____	Get your hair done.
_____	Get a massage.
_____	Go for a leisurely walk.
_____	Play your favorite music.
_____	Delight in your favorite hobby.
_____	Watch the sunset.
_____	Spend a day in bed when you're not sick.
_____	Eat a delicious treat.
_____	Burn a favorite scented candle or incense.
_____	See a play or Art film.
_____	Go hiking/biking.
_____	Jog or run.
_____	Watch a funny movie.
_____	Look through old photos.
_____	Read an engrossing book.
_____	Enjoy a fine wine.
_____	Do yoga.
_____	Play an instrument.
_____	Paint or sculpt.

_____	Go to a museum.
_____	Dance.
_____	Nap.
_____	
_____	
_____	
_____	

Using this list as a reference, check off only things that make you feel special. Now make a list of additional activities that appeal to you in the spaces provided above.

Finally

Choose at least one nurturing act per day and do it. In the beginning you may have to coax yourself, but hopefully soon you will learn to enjoy nurturing yourself, and even take pleasure from the process of choosing and then checking things off the list. Real change is more likely to happen if it is planned ahead and put in writing.

In the grid below, plan a weeks worth of nurturing activities. Choose one for each day of the week. Mix them up; some days choose passive activities, and on others choose physically activities.

Sunday	
Monday	
Tuesday	
Wednesday	

Thursday	
Friday	
Saturday	

I would like to leave you with some thoughts on finding your quiet place via spiritual practices that will renew you. Your relationship with that something sacred that is deep within you needs time spent thinking or praying. Contemplative reflection keeps you in touch with the soul. Spiritual practices can range from organized religion to more informal eclectic practices like: yoga, tai chi, guided imagery, biofeedback, journaling, retreats, and visualization.

Please remember, good time management does not mean working every possible moment of everyday. The best performers understand the need for routine relaxation. It is wise to build in small downtimes to avoid a large one, such as illness. So be wise, take time to be quiet. We are, after all, human *beings,* not doings, so try *being* more by doing less.

I hope you have learned that there are limitless ways to escape when life's demands overwhelm. The only limit is your imagination and willingness to employ some of the techniques shared in this chapter.

Seek out your own quiet place and make it yours. You have today and you have yourself. Now you also have the road map to find your quiet place. Use it in peace and enjoy your journey.

ABOUT THE AUTHOR

MARY PAUL

Mary Paul is the Senior Organization Development and Training Manager for Harley-Davidson Motor Company's Powertrain Operations and Juneau Avenue Corporate Headquarters in Milwaukee Wisconsin. Mary's primary responsibilities include taking a leadership role in the design and development of organizational change efforts that are consistent with evolving organizational needs and business requirements. She also assists in the development of strategies for the provides coaching to Harley-Davidson Leadership to identify training needs and create appropriate actions to meet those needs to support the organization's stratigic plan.

Prior to her current role, Mary has held several positions within Harley-Davidson, including being a Program Manager for Rider's Edge Motorcycle Training program, plus various positions within the Organization Development and Training Department.

In the past, Mary has also held management positions with Anheuser-Busch Companies and Sara Lee in St. Louis, Missouri.

Committed to her profession, Mary is also a member of a number of professional business organizations including The Professional Woman Network, Professional Dimensions, Women in Networking, and the American Society for Training and Development.

Contact
Organization Development and Training Manager
Harley-Davidson Motor Company
5801 S. Oak Road
West Bend, WI 53095
(414) 343-4652
mary.paul@harley-davidson.com

EIGHTEEN

SAYING NO WITHOUT GUILT

By Mary Paul

When Linda Eastman first asked me to write this chapter, my first thought was to say no. I really didn't have the time, and I was the poster child for saying "yes" to almost every request. But, I couldn't say no to Linda, either. Besides, I considered her not only a business colleague, but also a friend. What if I said **no** to writing the chapter and she became upset with me? What if I broke the trust she had in me? What if she didn't ask me to remain on the Professional Woman's Network Board? It never occurred to me that she might just say, "Thank you, I know that you are busy", and go on to another possible author.

I went on to obsess over the chapter for several months, procrastinating to the last minute, because I did not want to deal with my inner feelings of saying yes to another request. I was overwhelmed at my job, with committee work in several professional organizations, and family obligations. It came to me about a month before the editing deadline that I was the perfect author for this chapter, "How to Say

No Without (too much) Guilt". Especially since I seldom say no, and suffer from loads of self-induced guilt.

My coach, Roberta Colasanti, whom I'll interview in this chapter often, called me, *"Yes with feet."* The picture that conjured up in my mind fit me perfectly. I would run from meeting to meeting, event to event, family member to family member, and walk away with a laundry list of assignments and favors to do for others. If I did beg off, I felt guilty for not being there when someone needed me, or feeling like I was not pulling my weight. At the same time, I was angry with myself, and felt resentful towards those I had said yes to, because I neglected in taking care of my own personal needs for renewal.

Good grief, I'm 54 years old! Why am I having so much inner turmoil with saying no! I could easily find things or people to blame for my inability to say no without guilt. I decided to turn to an expert, my coach, Roberta Colasanti. Roberta and I have had many hours of coaching sessions devoted to my overwhelming tendency to say yes automatically to the vast majority of requests. I asked Roberta if I could interview her on her findings in working with women, like myself, who have a difficult time in saying no. I believe she puts into context why saying no is part of the "Superwoman Syndrome".

An Interview with Roberta Colasanti

1. **In your work and research, have you found that many women today have difficulty saying no to requests?**

"In my twenty-three years as a psychotherapist, I regularly have female patients who seek assistance specifically due to how challenging or intimidating it feels for them to decline requests. This is in striking contrast to the fact that, in all the years of my clinical practice, I cannot recall one male patient seeking help for his inability to say no to requests.

Women seek therapy because they recognize how their inability to decline requests keeps them harried, exhausted, and anxious. They see how their need to say yes is based on a fundamental belief that they are to please and be nice. They seek treatment when they recognize that their challenge declining requests comes at great cost to them. Accepting all requests compromises their time for themselves, and can contribute to resentment and dissatisfaction in their relationships."

2. **Is this prevalent only in North American culture, or have you seen saying no a problem in other cultures as well?**

"Although I do have a culturally diverse practice, I must say that I primarily work with women who have been raised in the United States. As a first generation Italian-American myself, I do attract many first generation women in my practice. I do assess that women born outside of the U.S., as well as those whose parents have been born overseas, appear to have greater difficulty declining requests. This inability to see and act from greater choice regarding accepting or declining requests appears to me to be very culturally based.

The Women's Movement in the United States clearly raised our collective consciousness about increasing the choices and the roles of women in modern society. This started as a uniquely American phenomenon that has impacted women worldwide. However, our American culture has created the environment and context that appears to make it more possible for women in the US to challenge traditional roles and expectations.

I find culturally that I do see women of Asian, Middle Eastern, and European descent having greater difficultly declining requests. These women are more likely to feel the lack of choice regarding requests. Cultures that foster subservient attitudes regarding women are those that tend to make declining requests all the more challenging for women. It is often seen as the woman's role to not only accept all requests, but to also actively anticipate what is needed by others, and know how to offer it before it is even asked.

I recall as a child and throughout my growing up years, that my grandmother, who was born and raised in Italy, seemed clairvoyant to me in her capacity to anticipate and provide what all family members required without having to be asked. She would actually feel as though she was not doing her job if her immediate family had to actually get to the point in which they had to ask for they wanted. Her role as the caregiver, as so many women experience, was to give without question, and to give no matter what sacrifice may have been required from her.

The role of female as caregiver appears quite fundamental to me across all cultures, and is a significant factor in what determines why women have such difficulty declining requests without enormous guilt. One feels guilty if she thinks she is falling down on the job. If the job of caregiver has been predestined and unquestioned, then one can see how guilt is a natural by-product of saying no."

3. What is triggered for women when they say no?

"People often interpret the reason women do not say no is because they feel guilty if they do not accept requests. Therefore, I think it is a valuable inquiry to question what is meant by the phenomenon of guilt. I interpret guilt as the feeling that is generated when a person does not meet another person's standards or expectations. We feel guilty saying no if we think we are supposed to say yes, or because we fear we will upset another. As mentioned in the previous question, the role of women as caregivers provides an inherent standard of providing what others require and to do so without question.

Concern for whether or not one has met another person's standards indicates to me that such an individual may be missing or disregarding their own standards for the sake of the other. Women, who automatically say yes, even when they want to decline, seem to be more motivated by others' assessments of them. This need to have other's approval and positive assessments in order to feel good about herself particularly compromises the development of a whole and authentic self. Human beings do not develop a strong inner experience of self if one's attention is primarily focused on how others perceive them.

I assess that we manage guilt with greater authenticity when we are living from our own personal guidelines and standards. Personal standards orient us to the actions that are acceptable to us. We can extend better to others when we first plant ourselves firmly in our own standards. When an individual knows who they are and what they stand for, it makes it much easier to accept or decline requests with dignity. If one has to say yes to all requests in order to avoid the feelings that guilt generates, then that person is never really saying yes. The fear of declining requests based on what other's will think of you keeps the "self" imprisoned, and one is then acting from servitude instead of authenticated adulthood. Adulthood, for me, is the capacity to accept all consequences generated in life by living by one's own standards and expectations."

4. **Given the fact that a woman has difficulty in saying no, are there alternative strategies she can use to cope with the desire of wanting to say yes to requests?**

"Since automatically saying yes is coupled with the lack of personal standards, I feel this is a key area in which to begin. I work with my clients to help them determine and live from personal standards. I see my role as a therapist as helping my clients access and act from their full adulthood.

I often share with my clients that "Being comes before Doing." How and who they wish to **Be** in life should determine what they **Do**. We often have this backwards. Many people, especially those motivated by not wanting to feel uncomfortable feelings such as guilt or shame, stay very busy and in a "doing-mode" in order to feel like they have "Be-come" something.

I also feel that one can get very flooded with the feelings of guilt that are generated when risking saying no. Therefore, I teach Mindfulness Practice as a means of helping to self-regulate one's system. Mindfulness is simply the capacity to observe one's feelings instead of participating with them. Guilt is a feeling. Feelings have the powerful capacity to inform us about ourselves and our standards. Often, especially for women who have difficulty declining requests, feelings are used to *determine* instead of *inform* behavior. Having one's feelings determine behavior compromises one's capacity to bring forth a full and authentic sense of self.

My clients use Mindfulness practice to observe their historic desire to say yes, but instead of acting on the feeling to say yes, they learn how to observe it. They literally watch themselves. Learning how to be the witness to their desire to say yes, allows them to be informed by it. They can notice the historic and automatic behavior to want to say yes, and they learn that what they feel is informing them of this. Coupling this observing capacity with the ability to act from clear personal intentions, the automatic desire to say yes no longer has to run the show.

I also use the model of Speech Act Theory in my practice. Without getting into a lengthy discussion of this model, it will suffice to say that women learn to negotiate, which includes making a counter-offer instead of accepting to do all that is being asked of them. They learn to "commit-to-commit," meaning specifying a later time when she will accept or decline the request. This tactic allows her to consider whether meeting the request is consistent with her standards, and to reflect upon the time required to actually fulfill the request. This tactic increases the woman's ability to make more rigorous assessments as to whether or not she can really fulfill the request within the time frame that is being asked of her. Women who automatically say yes often also fall into the trap of underestimating what is truly required to fulfill a promise. She does not fully take into account how much time is necessary to complete what is being asked of her. This can increase feelings of guilt when the request is accepted, only to be compromised when not completed in a timely manner. Women who have difficulty saying no often risk actually making good on their promises, because they have so over-extended themselves that they can not possibly fulfill all that has been requested within the agreed timeframe. This only heightens feelings of guilt and inadequacy. Therefore, learning how to commit-to-commit provides one with the space necessary to fully assess what is being asked, whether it fits into one's standards to fulfill and the time required to actually completing the request in relationship to all other outstanding promises."

5. **This is a difficult behavior to break. What advice do you have to help women make it through the tendency of falling back into old patterns of saying yes?**

"It is critically important to be clear about one's intention to have greater choice when faced with a request. Learning to say no is a skill that has to be practiced. Like any new behavior, it takes time to become proficient. Being patient with one's self and tolerating the discomfort that arises is part of the learning process. As I indicated above, Mindfulness allows us to observe the awkwardness and the impulse to return to familiar behaviors without acting on them. As with all learning, we become proficient when our neural pathways have been altered by practice and repetition over time. In a culture of impatience and quick fixes, it is helpful to remind ourselves that learning something new takes time and practice.

Roberta Colasanti is a licensed psychotherapist and principal of Colasanti and Associates, located in Boston, MA. Ms. Colasanti is one of the creators of the "Ways to Wellness" program, which focuses on mind-body medicine and its connection with emotional and physical stress. Ms. Colasanti was associated with the Harvard Community Health Plan, a Harvard Medical School – affiliated health maintenance organization prior to opening her own practice.

As you can see from Roberta's remarks, there are many of us plagued with saying yes to requests when we really want to say no.

One of the first steps I have taken in learning to say no is to counter-offer. Using a counter-offer such as, "I may be able to, however I need to check my workload", gives me a little time to truly evaluate the request and protect my resources. Of course, the important thing is to get back to the person who made the request in a timely manner, regardless of whether your response is yes or no. However, I realize that I am in control of my timing in responding, and use Mindfulness to calm any anxiety I may encounter over not responding "yes" immediately to their requests.

It's important to be patient with yourself, because it take's practice, strength, and the ability to know that in the long run, you and your sanity will benefit from saying no. I've found that people that I have said "no" to even respect me more. Many have confided that they are glad I'm finally taking care of myself first; they know that I can then better take care of the needs of others.

Talk to your friends, find a life coach, see a counselor and talk out any angst you may have with saying no to requests from others. I discovered that respecting my own wishes has given me a new sense of well being, and ready to take on new challenges in my life."

Illustration by Judith Casey

ABOUT THE AUTHOR

RUBY M. ASHLEY, MBA

Ruby Ashley is Chief Executive Officer of Ruby Ashley & Associates. She is a leader in personal and professional development, specializing in the delivery of workshops, seminars, training programs, and assessments. Her workshops and training programs are highly interactive and stimulating with focus on improving employee performance. She firmly believes that as long as individuals are willing to learn, change, and grow, they will always reach high levels of achievement.

Ms. Ashley is an accomplished motivational keynote speaker, facilitator, trainer, and consultant with more than 26 years of experience in the corporate environment. As a Certified Customer Service Trainer, she delivers an outstanding Customer Service Excellence program. Other training program topics include: personal and professional development, women's issues, diversity and multiculturalism, self-esteem, leadership development, strategic planning, road map to retirement, and team building. Teen topics are Save Our Youth, Teen Image, and Leadership.

Ms. Ashley earned Bachelor's and Master's degrees in Business from Brenau University in Gainesville, GA. She is a member of The Professional Woman Network (PWN), is a certified trainer, and member of The PWN International Advisory Board. Ms. Ashley holds memberships in other professional organizations, including the American Business Woman Association, Toastmasters International, Les Brown Speaker's Bureau, and is an affiliate of Leadership Development Group, Inc. She is a youth mentor and an active volunteer in her community.

Ruby Ashley is also a co-author of *Becoming the Professional Woman, Self-Esteem & Empowerment for Women* and *The Young Woman's Guide for Personal Success* in the PWN Library.

Contact
Ruby Ashley & Associates
1735 Chatham Ridge Circle #206
Charlotte, NC 28273
(404) 316-5931
rbyash@aol.com
www.protrain.net

NINETEEN

WHO ARE YOU?

By Ruby Ashley

Self-Definition

Many times people describe/define themselves based upon their roles or careers. In answer to the question, "Who Are You?", a typical response might be: "Jim's daughter", "Mark's wife", "Carla's mom", or a lawyer/receptionist/teacher, etc. Although these titles may define who you are in terms of your relationship with others (or your job), they aren't really the *essence* of you. In order to really understand who you are, you have to go deep inside yourself to understand your value system and your core beliefs. The search for self can take you down many paths and can lead you in directions that may be painful, especially when you have to deal with unpleasant memories and past mistakes. However, the journey is an important one, which can lead to the realization of who you really are and your true purpose in life.

Past Perspective

"Who are you?" is a haunting question that, when answered with truth and honesty, can lead you to a deeper understanding of the real meaning of your life. But the question is not always an easy one. Often you will recall errors in judgment, which may have caused great pain to yourself or others. Other times you will remember unwelcome life changes that left you feeling shattered and unable to recover from the devastation. These life changes may include something that was a part of your identity, or someone who gave your life meaning and now is gone. It's important to have an understanding that life incidents will happen, mishaps will occur, and wrong choices will be made. As long as you are alive, you will face unforeseen, unfamiliar, and life-altering trials. However, no matter how great the pain you experience, when you look back, you must be able to reconcile your past, since it is a part of who you are. Even though it is not possible to change what happened yesterday, it is important to put the past in its proper perspective so that you can move on to your future.

For tomorrow only come once, and then it, to is gone.

Authentic Self

If you feel your life's journey thus far has been difficult and unkind, try to think of your past self as your fictional self. Why? Because your reactions to and interpretations of the negative experiences you've had in the past may have pulled you away from your authentic self – the person you truly are. When you conform to the pressure to be someone other than your true self, you lose touch with what makes you special. If that has happened to you, now is the time for you to step up and be the person you are really meant to be. Start by taking the actions necessary to reclaim your authentic self. As Jewel Diamond Taylor, motivational speaker and author states, "Knowledge is 'potential power.' Only action produces results."

Unique Differences

Everyone is different. Have you ever thought about what this world would be like if we all looked alike, spoke the same language, walked exactly the same way, and acted like everyone else? It would really be a boring place. Even though you may hear someone comment, "Hey, you look just like someone I know," or "I think you have a twin," it is really just an expression. Nobody is exactly like anyone else. We were all born with unique looks, gifts, and talents that belong to each of us. Even identical twins have many distinct characteristics. Despite the fact they look alike, they often have completely different personalities. Your differences make you unique and are important components of your authentic self.

Self-Awareness

In order to be true to your authentic self, you must become aware of your unique qualities and characteristics. A thorough self-analysis will help you see clearly the essence of who you are. Understanding your thoughts, feelings, and actions will enable you to change a negative attitude into a more positive one. Being able to deal with your feelings is important. When you suppress or repress your feelings, you often lose the ability to express how you truly feel. Are you the type of person who pushes your wants, needs, and feelings aside when trying to please others? If so, you should be aware that repressed feelings can lead to alcoholism, substance abuse, and other destructive behaviors.

Personal Example

In Orlando, Florida in 2004, I attended a speaker's conference. On my way to the conference, I learned that everyone attending would be speaking on Saturday and that the speech had to be ten minutes or less. I was not satisfied with the speech I had prepared, because I felt I didn't have a personal story that would fit the occasion. So I chose a topic that I wasn't really ready to deliver. As a result, when we did the practice run on Friday, I knew I didn't do very well. Because all the other speakers seemed so good and so polished, it took all the confidence I had to stand up and give my unprepared speech. Needless to say, that was the longest ten minutes I've ever encountered while speaking! When I left the stage, my confidence shaken, I had almost decided not to participate in the Saturday event. After I returned to my room, I was pacing back and forth questioning myself and my intentions. It was decision-making time, and I immediately came to the conclusion that I would not give up; instead, I was determined to go back the next day and give a good presentation. Determined, I began to prepare and made sure my speech was within the ten-minute time limit. The next day, after giving my speech, one of the speakers in the audience asked how I could have done so badly on Friday and then come back to do so well on Saturday. My response was, "I don't know who that was yesterday, but today, that was me." I am very much aware of who I am. I am not perfect, yet I continue to strive to become better and better. I've had some setbacks, but I took Willie Jolley's book to heart: *A Setback Is a Setup for a Comeback.* (I had the opportunity to meet Mr. Jolley at the Orlando conference.) What I ultimately learned from this experience was that no matter what we do, we must first believe in ourselves. Yes, even when we fail.

> *"People become really quite remarkable when they start thinking that they can do things. When they believe in themselves, they have the first secret of success."*
> — Norman Vincent Peale

Who Are You?

Exercise 1

Think of a challenging time in your life, a time when you questioned yourself and who you really are. Describe what happened and what you ultimately learned from the experience.

_____

_____

_____

_____

_____

_____

_____

_____

_____

Life Is A J-O-U-R-N-E-Y

Reflecting on past experiences can be very beneficial in helping people understand what made them who they are today. So, in a quiet place, I took a journey into my past. I could remember as far back as when I was 4-years old. I was surprised at the range of emotions I experienced — from laughter to sadness, thinking about both my good and bad choices, and how some of my dreams as a child are now realities. I also remembered people who will always be a part of my identity, though they are no longer a part of my life. During my journey, it was important that I acknowledged all of my feelings along the way. I journeyed among my past memories for quite a while, longer than I thought I would, and was surprised by how I felt at the end. Though I have achieved a great deal in my life so far, I feel the need to pick up the pace and keep moving to accomplish other goals. I know I need to stay focused on my dreams and aspirations, so I will continue to grow and become the person I was meant to be. I truly believe life is a journey and not a destination. It is a process with varied learning experiences, which continues throughout our lives. Often the journey takes place in stages. Some of the typical stages, according to the U.S. Census Bureau, are as follows:

The Stages of Life	
Life Phase: Immaturity → Maturity	
Youth	
Age	Stage
1-4	Early childhood
5-13	Elementary School
14-17	High School
18-22	Vocational school/college
23-25	First jobs
26-30	Gain real-world knowledge; invest in yourself
Adulthood	Advances career; develop
Age	Stage
31-40	Advances career; develop
41-50	Apply expertise in career and community
51-55	Enjoy lifestyle; mature career
56-65	Legacy established; retirement

Older Adulthood	
Age	Stage
66-75	Continued contributions, expertise, and relationships
76-84	Elder Statesperson
85+	Enjoy Life

Who Are You?

Exercise 2

Find a quiet place and go on a journey into your past. Answer the following questions, based on events from your journey.

In which of the 4 Stages of Life so far have you been the happiest?____

Why? _____

In which Stage of Life have you experienced a lot of pain? _____

Why? _____

In which Stage of Life did you experience major changes in your life?

_____

Explain_____

_____

In which stage of life thus far have you learned the most about life? __

Explain_____

_____

Self-Acceptance

Acceptance means you acknowledge what is. Self-acceptance means you recognize all your faults as well as all your positive qualities and character traits. Self-acceptance requires a willingness to acknowledge what is real without any denial — you think what you think, feel what you feel, desire what you desire, and have done what you have done. Simply stated, you are who you are. Rather than reject or disown any part of yourself, including your body, emotions, thoughts, or actions, acknowledge all the facts about yourself. Accepting yourself does not mean you approve or disapprove, it simply means that you accept who you are right now. Self-acceptance is so important because, if you can't accept who you are, it will be almost impossible to become the person you want to be.

True Expression

Be real with yourself and be willing to admit that even your negative emotions or behaviors are a true expression of you. You don't have to like or admire this part of who you are, but it's important to recognize that it is a part of you. Know that you have options to change any negativity you find, but for now, be real with yourself and have respect for the person you are. Self-acceptance is the precondition of change and growth, so why is it so hard for us to move on when we make mistakes? Perhaps it's because we haven't thought about the fact that we can't discover life's answers until we have experienced both failure and success.

Who Are You?

Exercise 3
Write a definition that will best describe who you are:

_____

_____

_____

Change, Change, Change

None of us will journey through life without knowing joy and pain, laughter and tears, hope and despair. We will encounter success, failure, accolades, insults, and change on top of more change. All will have an effect on **who you are**. Change is action. You can never completely change all of who you are, but if you are unhappy, make some important adjustments by exercising your choice to change (i.e. leave a maladaptive career or abusive marriage) and find a whole new life. Be bold and change your regular routine. Make an appointment for a day at the spa, sign up for a yoga/exercise class, or spend the day volunteering.

> *"Our lives are not determined by what happens to us*
> *but by how we react to what happens,*
> *not by what life brings us,*
> *but by the attitude we bring to life.*
> *A positive attitude causes a chain reaction*

Of positive thoughts, events, and outcomes.
It is a catalyst, a spark that creates extraordinary results."
— Anonymous

"Who are you?" ultimately is a question which can only be answered by you and you alone. Take a good look at yourself, and if you don't like what you see, make some changes. It's never too late to become the person you are meant to be. It is up to you. Just make up your mind to be the best person you can be with the most positive attitude you can have. Then the next time you question who you are, you will find you are happy with the answer.

Notes:

ABOUT THE AUTHOR

LaWanda S Dudley

LaWanda S Dudley is Founder and the Chief Executive Officer, of The SmithDudley Group, an organization specializing in empowerment seminars for women, young adults, and youth. She has more than ten years of professional experience. As a former Flight Attendant, she traveled and explored different cultures and is committed to educating individuals on the importance of diverse corporate cultures, business etiquette, professional image and maintaining a positive attitude. The SmithDudley Group was founded in 2005, created to motivate, inspire, encourage, and empower individuals to make positive changes in their life.

Ms. Dudley was educated in a universal setting; experiencing the unique challenges faced by today's women, young adults, and youth. Her determination to make a difference motivated her desire to fulfill the need for empowering and building the self esteem necessary to achieve greater mental, physical, spiritual and emotional health.

Ms. Dudley has a BS in Management and is currently pursuing a MS in Counseling/Psychology. In addition to working as a volunteer in her community, she has facilitated workshops on Leadership, Professional/Teen Image, Perception and Self-Esteem. Ms. Dudley is an active member of The Professional Woman Network International Speakers Bureau.

Contact
LaWanda S Dudley
The SmithDudley Group, LLC
P. O. Box 610353
Birmingham, AL 35261
(205) 337-2428
lawanda@thesmithdudleygroup.com

TWENTY

ELIMINATING POISONOUS RELATIONSHIPS

By LaWanda S. Dudley

First, let's define a poisonous relationship; a poisonous relationship is any relationship that allows you not to be yourself. When we allow others to determine how we should feel or what we should say and do, we lose insight of our own self- identity. People come into our lives to teach us about ourselves. There is a saying that people come into our lives for a reason, season or a lifetime.

Each day of our lives, many of us focus on making others happy and getting their approval; we let others decide what to wear, what we drive, how big a house we should buy and who we are affiliated with. Our relationships with others have great impact as to how we feel about ourselves. Other people have the power to have us develop self -doubt, low self-esteem; question our confidence to perform and the inability to say "no" without feeling guilty.

How relationships become poison

Relationships become poisonous when you forget to take control of your life. You don't speak up! You continue saying that the relationship will get better, but you never do anything to change the situation. Why would you stay on a job you hate? Why remain in a marriage that is fallen apart? Why keep a friend who is never there for you? Perhaps it is because you are afraid to let go! Even if it is hurting us, we still hold on to the familiar. We have a habit of making excuses for all of the reason not to move on. But there comes a time when we must learn *how* to let go. When we are in a poisonous relationship, we tend to make poor decisions. We make decisions out of distress and anger; but instead, we must get in a quiet place and take an inward look for guidance. Relationships are meant to enhance, encourage and enrich our lives. Poisonous relationships do just the opposite; they are unhealthy and will take a toll on your mental, physical, emotional and financial state. And before you notice, you are in a big, deep mess!

Remember when you were a child and couldn't wait to grow up? You dressed up and pranced around the mirror, exploring how beautiful you looked. Life was simple, and it meant so much just to be able to imagine looking into that mirror and looking back at a healthy, vibrant child. When you look into the mirror now, what do you see? A relationship with another is the mirror image of the relationship with self. Look hard and concentrate on what image you see. The healthier you are emotionally and mentally, the better your chances of having a healthy relationship with others.

Exercise #1
My Relationship Chart
Complete the following:

Questions To Ask:	My worst memory	What I learned (Write a positive lesson.)	How to eliminate (Write a brief statement that will help you deal with the event and get on with your life.)
Who hurt me?			
Whom did I hurt?			
Who left me (what did I lose)?			
What opportunity did I miss?			
What mistake did I make?			

Exercise #2

Consider the following list. Here are ways that a relationship can become toxic: *Relationship Sabotage* (10 ways to sabotage a relationship.)

1. Don't allow yourself to be vulnerable.

2. Don't find ways to renew your relationship.

3. Don't share your values.

4. Worry only about your own growth.

5. Take the other person for granted.

6. Sacrifice your identity for the other person's gain.

7. Don't set mutual life goals.

8. Focus on the Me instead of the WE.

9. Never be willing to compromise.

10. Smother the other person (you determine whether that's literal or figurative).

Eliminating the Poisonous Relationship

Relationships are like flowers; they need nurturing, water, and sun to survive. Relationships need love, honesty, and commitment in order to continue to be positive. According to Dr. Mark J. Warner, "Relationships are an intriguing aspect of life. Because they are a study in contradictions, they produce paradoxical feelings ranging from clarity to confusion, from ecstasy to depression, from being on top of the world to being down in the dumps. Of course relationships change. They get better or they get worse, but they never stay the same. Relationships really are like a roller coaster, you have ups and downs." So you should ask yourself:

- Am I happy or unhappy most of the time in the relationship?

- How often do I have ups and downs?

- How much do I contribute to the ups?

- Am I doing everything to help the relationship survive?

It is poison when you surround yourself with people who have a different mind set about the goals that you have planned in your life. Many times we think the person will change and grow along with us. The people who don't share the same passion for your purpose will cause confusion. They will make your job unbearable, your marriage miserable, and destroy a friendship. (Although, it is improbable to always surround yourself with people who think *just* like you do. You need to be compatible and similar in areas of values to produce a lasting relationship.) Pastor T. D. Jakes tells us, "If you are going to be ultimately effective and maximize a relationship, you need people who have the same directional agreement. They may not do everything the way you do, but they must have the same directional thrust. They should be people who are on their way. People who have direction and goals understand commitment and tenacity. People who do not share your directional thrust are weights and albatrosses around your neck, and they will cause you to sink."

Exercise #3:

"Help me to know when the relationship is poison, and give me the strength to let go."

Write down the names of people who meet the following criteria:	
You like or love them.	**You value their advice.**
1.	1.
2.	2.
3.	3.
4.	4.
You trust their judgment.	**You'd let them borrow money.**
1.	1.
2.	2.
3.	3.
4.	4.
You respect their opinions.	**Their opinions are:**
1.	
2.	
3.	
4.	
5.	
6.	
7.	

Close your eyes and mentally review your relationships. As you revisit each relationship, make notes about the feeling your body exhibits when you think of them. Are you tense, relaxed, feeling warm and loved?

Person	Body Feeling
1.	
2.	
3.	
4.	

List the difficult relationships

- _____

- _____

- _____

- _____

- _____

Consider the relationships that bring on difficult feelings. Examine and write down what you have learned from these relationships, and what needs to change.

_____
_____
_____
_____

Decide how to move on. List ways that the relationship must change, or you will end it.

_____
_____
_____
_____

Write down your new approach to a poisonous relationship.

1. _____

2. _____

3. _____

4. _____

5. _____

Stewart D. Jackson: A Lesson In Life

Sometimes people come into your life and you know right away that they were meant to be there. They serve some sort of purpose, teach you a lesson, or help figure out who you are or who you want to become. You never know who these people may be: your roommate, neighbor, professor, long lost friend, lover, or even a complete stranger that, when you lock eyes with them, you know that very moment that they will affect your life in some profound way.

And sometimes things happen to you, and at the time they may seem horrible, painful and unfair, but in reflection you realize that, without overcoming those obstacles, you would have never realized your potential, strength, will power or heart.

Everything happens for a reason. Nothing happens by chance or by means of good or bad luck. Illness, injury, love, lost moments of true greatness, and sheer stupidity all occur to test the limits of your soul. Without these small tests, whether they be events, illness or relationships, life would be like a smoothly paved, straight, flat road to nowhere. Life would be safe and comfortable, but dull and utterly pointless.

The people you meet affect your life and the successes and downfalls you experience. They are the ones who create who you are. Even the bad experiences can be learned from... those lessons are the hardest and probably the most important ones.

If someone hurts you, betrays you, or breaks your heart, forgive them, for they have helped you learn about trust and the importance of being cautious to whom you open your heart.

If someone loves you, love them back unconditionally, not only because they love you, but also because they are teaching you to love, and opening your heart and eyes to things you would have never seen or felt without them.

Make every day count. Appreciate every moment, and take from it everything that you possibly can, for you may never be able to experience it again. Talk to people you have never talked to before, and actually listen. Let yourself fall in love, break free, and set your sights high. Hold your head up because you have every right to.

Tell yourself you are a great individual, and believe in yourself, for if you don't believe in yourself, no one else will believe in you, either.

You can make of your life anything you wish. Create you own life, and then go out and live it!

ABOUT THE AUTHOR

DR. MAMIE SHIELDS NORMAN

Dr. Mamie Shields Norman is the library media specialist and technology coordinator at Thomas Johnson Middle School in Lanham, Maryland, Prince George's County Public Schools. She serves as adjunct faculty at Sojourner-Douglass College in Annapolis, Maryland, and is the owner/CEO of The Shields Group, LLC, an educational and personal development consulting firm.

Dr. Shields Norman owns and operates a pre-K Montessori weekend school. She has presented various workshops on early childhood and independence in the very young child. During 2004 Dr. Norman was a presenter at the Professional Woman Network International Conference in Louisville, Kentucky, and served on the 2005 Woman Network International Advisory Board.

Before returning to the library profession, Dr. Shields Norman taught pre-K Montessori for eight years. She has been an educator for 38 years and is committed to the education of children, youth and adults, encouraging them to reach their highest potential and become all they can be.

Certification in the following areas qualifies Dr. Shields Norman to be of great service to many: Leadership Skills for Women, Becoming the Assertive Woman, Self-esteem and Self-empowerment, pre-K Montessori, and Anger Management for Young People.

Dr. Sheilds Norman is a native of Memphis Tennessee and the sixth child of seven. She currently resides in Bowie, Maryland with her two sons, Yohance and Zikomo. Dr. Shields Norman holds a Bachelor's degree in Sociology form Tuskegee University, a Master's in Library Science from Atlanta University, a Master's in Elementary Education from American International College, a Master's in Guidance and Psychological Services from Springfield College, and is AMI-certified as pre-K Montessori.

Contact
The Shields Group, LLC
15480 Annapolis Road Ste. 202 #258
Bowie, MD 20715
mshields2@verizon.net
www.protrain.net

TWENTY-ONE

SETTING BOUNDARIES IN YOUR LIFE

By Dr. Mamie Shields-Norman

Would you allow someone to enter your home and remove some of your possessions without complaining? Their actions of entering your home have invaded your personal boundaries. They have invaded your space. Today, more than ever, we hear discussions about boundaries; when, where and how to set them. In this chapter, we will take a brief look at how to set boundaries in your life.

When we think about setting boundaries, we think about placing limits on how far a person can go with another person.

The essence of setting boundaries is to put a controlling behavior of another person in check. If we do not put such individuals in check, they can rule and control our very lives. When we are in relationship with someone who exhibits controlling behaviors, this may weaken the boundaries we have established.

Why are boundaries important? Boundaries are important because it says to yourself and to others that I have self-respect, and I expect you to respect me. To set and maintain boundaries requires some work, strength, determination, and most important, the desire.

How could this be? Well, if we stop for a minute and think about you, your life, and the people who surround you, what is it that you DESIRE? For most of us the main DESIRE is to be HAPPY! So, from this DESIRE to be happy, we have to look at all those things, people and situations that, we believe, will make us happy.

Can you list the ten things or circumstances that create the DESIRE for you to be happy?

1. _____

2. _____

3. _____

4. _____

5. _____

6. _____

7. _____

8. _____

9. _____

10. _____

Now that you have listed all of the circumstances that will create DESIRE for you to be happy, the next step is to set boundaries in your life to ensure your happiness. You ensure your happiness by not allowing others to control and manipulate your life. If this occurs, then you no longer have control over what happens in your life. You can lose your whole life to these controlling individuals. Therefore, boundaries must be in place to prevent this from happening.

It is important to have boundaries in our lives because, without boundaries we are saying to others that they are allowed to treat us anyway they wish, and nothing will be done about it. It is a clear message to others that you have no respect for yourself, and that you do not value your life. Take a look at some of the boundaries you currently have or do not have; consider what you allow and do not allow to happen to you.

1. Do you allow important people in your life to put you down? _____

2. Do you set limits as to how far other can go? Do you draw the line? _____

3. Do you allow others to take advantage of you?_____

4. Do you feel excluded from your friends or others because you have set boundaries? _____

5. Do you accept treatment that would devalue you and lower your self-esteem? _____

6. Do you withhold expressing your feelings to persons who violate your personhood and try to control your feelings, choices, behavior and values?_____

7. Do you shy away from relationships because you are afraid to set boundaries? _____

8. Do you fear setting boundaries with those who are close to you because you do not want to hurt their feelings?_____

9. Do you know when to say NO in a situation? How do you feel afterwards? _____

10. _____
_____

11. Do you know when to say YES in a situation? How do you feel afterwards? _____

12. _____
_____

13. Would you allow someone to enter your home and remove some of your possession without complaining? _____

How do you set boundaries in your life? First, we must understand that boundaries are very important in our lives. Let us take a look at five categories of boundaries:

1. **No boundaries** – Having no boundaries is not a good place to be. Having

2. no boundaries means that others are allowed to impose upon your privacy,

3. and allow your space to be violated.

4. **Stiff boundaries** – Having boundaries that will not allow others to get to know you or you exhibit behavior that says, "Stay away!" These boundaries show little feelings and emotions in relationships.

5. **Emotional boundaries** – Having sensitivity or insensitivity to the feelings of others.

6. **Healthy boundaries** – Having boundaries that are expressed and made clear to others, which shows respect for yourself and others.

7. **Unhealthy boundaries** – Having boundaries that are not expressed and made clear to others, which show disrespect for yourself and others.

Boundaries allow us space to look at life and see how we are going to function effectively as we live our lives. Boundaries protect us from being harmed by others, and especially those we care about and who care about us. From childhood, we have been taught how to set boundaries, and from childhood our parents were the first persons who introduced us to boundary setting. When our parents set limits, developed rules of the home, they were setting the framework in which to teach us about life and how to function within the rules of life. (And when our parents lived *without boundaries* such as abusive behavior, swearing and hitting, alcoholism, or adultery, we witnessed lack of boundaries, and how that affected our parents and ourselves.) So, all through our lives, we either have learned how to set boundaries and have done so, or we have learned how to set boundaries and did not because of the controlling behavior of others. In other words, setting boundaries is a choice we make. It is in our best interest and for our well being that we set boundaries in all aspects of our lives. Setting boundaries shows respect for ourselves and protects us from being used.

Take a few moments to look at the boundaries you have set in your life and see if they are healthy. List ten boundaries you have set in your life:

1. _____

2. _____

3. _____

4. _____

5. _____

6. _____

7. _____

8. _____

9. _____

Who have you witnessed during your lifetime who allowed others to invade their boundaries or invaded other's boundaries? Who and what happened?

1. _____

2. _____

3. _____

4. _____

5. _____

What could they have done differently to stop someone from invading their boundaries (or been respectful enough not to invade some else's boundaries).

1. _____

2. _____

3. _____

4. _____

5. _____

If the boundaries you have set for your life are not healthy, below are five steps you can follow as you learn how to set healthy boundaries:

1. You must be motivated or have the **desire** to set healthy boundaries in your life. You have already listed 10 boundaries. Now, look and see if these boundaries have been violated and how this has affected your life. Record your feelings about the violation(s).

_____

_____

_____

2.   Take a look at what situations led to the violation of your boundaries. Ask yourself if the boundaries set were strong enough, and how you allowed them to be violated?

_____

_____

_____

3.   Next, look at your unhealthy situations and see how you can make immediate corrections without experiencing further violation of your boundaries.

_____

_____

_____

4.   Surround yourself with positive people in all of your relationships at home, work, social events, community and religious work. Do not allow yourself to be in the company of controlling people as you build or rebuild your set of boundaries. List a few settings where you need change:

_____

_____

_____

5.   Connect with people who have set clear boundaries for their lives and begin to develop relationships with them. This is so important, because we need to surround ourselves with people who share the same values and set boundaries for their lives. Being in relationship with people who set boundaries is reinforcement for you, as well as support.

As you practice setting boundaries, you will find that it is not an easy task to accomplish. You will find yourself using words such as, "I don't' feel good when you......", " No, I don't want you talking to me that way!", "If you do that again, then I will........". You are in the process of moving from life without boundaries to a life with boundaries (and a new "Boundary Vocabulary). In some cases, you may disconnect from current relationships; people will notice a change and great difference in your life. If they are controlling, they may stop associating with you, because they can no longer have control over you.

Setting boundaries is a work in progress. Life will become totally different. You will begin to feel a sense of freedom. You will begin to like yourself more, and value who you are, and so will others. When you get your life back and have a sense of freedom, you will find that Freedom and Boundaries are really synonymous. People may think of boundaries as being like a fence, penning you in. But instead, the boundaries you will now place in your life will be the "Emotional Protection" that you need to be certain that they do not cross over the line and harm you in any way. You will learn to protect yourself. At the same time, understanding that everyone deserves respect, you will also become more aware of how important it is not to cross other's boundaries.

May you live a life filled with invisible yet powerful boundaries that will always protect you both emotionally and physically.

ABOUT THE AUTHOR

Dr. Madeline Ann Lewis

Dr. Lewis is President/CEO of the Deline Institute for Professional Development. She conducts workshops and seminars that have been presented throughout the United States and abroad. Specializing in Women's Issues, Dr. Lewis is a passionate believer in self-esteem, desiring to guide women to achieve their best mental, physical, spiritual and emotional health. She is an accomplished keynote speaker, facilitator, consultant, trainer and coach.

Dr. Lewis' knowledge of business and professionalism stems from twenty one years of military service and nineteen years as a civilian in Federal government. Dr. Lewis is an adjunct professor for National-Louis University and University of Phoenix. Dr. Lewis is listed in Manchester Who's Who for Executives and Professionals, as well as Metropolitan Who's Who for demonstrating outstanding leadership in her profession. She hold membership with several organizations such as: Professional Woman Speakers Bureau, National Association for Female Executives, Federally Employed Women, African American Federal Executives Association and serves on the International Advisory Board of the Professional Woman Network.

She appeared in the National Association of Female Executives Magazine Success (Fall Issue 2005) titled "Military Moxie" and on Radio One Talk Show, A Woman's Journey to Success, Topic: *Superwoman Syndrome.*

Among her accolades, is a governor's citation from former Maryland Governor William Shaffer (for service during Desert Storm), three Attorney General's Volunteer Service Awards and a Director's Award for Outstanding Foreign Counterintelligence Investigation from the FBI. Dr. Lewis was nominated for the Office Depot 2007 Business Woman of the Year Award.

Dr. Lewis has written articles titled: *Making the Deal: Women as Negotiators; Playing from the Blue Tees: Women in the Federal Government; How Women Can Speed Progress on Diversity at Work and How to Get the Promotion you Deserve,* which appeared in business journals, Federal magazines and college websites.

She is also the co-author of **A Women's Journey to Wellness: Mind, Body and Spirit.**

Contact
Deline Institute for Professional Development
P.O. Box 5091
Capitol Heights, MD 20791
(301) 693-3284
sioc@aol.com
www.protrain.net/lewis.htm
www.delineinstitute.net

TWENTY-TWO

MIRROR! MIRROR! TAKING A STRESS INVENTORY

By Dr. Madeline Ann Lewis

Introduction

What rhymes with "mess," has six letters, and has no business in your life? Stress! If you're like most people, stress has a way of creeping into your life and trying to make a mess of things. You encounter stress at work and at home, in traffic, at the grocery store, even when you're watching television or listening to the radio. (Seems like it's hard to get away from it, doesn't it?) That may be true, but you do have the power at hand to minimize stress in your life, even to replace "bad stress" with "good stress."

Is there such a thing as "good stress?" You bet! When you exercise, for example, you put stress on your muscles, and this is a good thing because, over time, this form of stress helps build your muscles and make you stronger. But what happens if you exercise perpetually without taking a break? Your body can't take it, and you break down. You need a sufficiently long recovery period in between workouts in order for good stress to be effective; otherwise it'll quickly turn into bad stress.

Stress is also good when it comes in the form of a boost of adrenalin that gets you out of the way of a speeding car, or when it pumps you up so you can give a dynamite presentation, or score that soccer goal. Good stress is short-lived and propels you toward a specific goal. Bad stress, on the other hand, is excessive and even chronic. You don't get a break from it, and you break down at some level—physically, emotionally, mentally, or all of the above. Part of your job is to look in the mirror, so to speak, and recognize the difference between these two kinds of stress in your life and how they affect you. Then you can take attainable steps to minimize your exposure to long-term, harmful stress, and maximize your health and wellbeing.

What Is Stress?

Stress, as we commonly know it, describes the mental, physical, and emotional tension we experience when exposed to different forms of stimuli. What one person regards as stress may not be stress at all for someone else. Look at two people going on a rollercoaster ride, for example. One absolutely loves it and has a fantastic time, while the other experiences pure torture. The way each of us responds to stress is highly individualistic. One person might scream, another might hold everything inside, and a third might figure out a way to not let stress get to them. How you deal with stress depends on many factors, including your personality type, past experiences, tolerance levels, even how much sleep you had the night before.

One thing's certain: The same modern-day complexity that gives us more choices, more opportunities, and even greater comforts than ever before, also presents us with more stressors on a day-to-day basis. Stressors are those external and internal factors that produce stress in our lives. You know, things like deadlines, traffic jams, sensational news reports, the dishwasher leaking, the dog throwing up on the carpet again.

The good news is that, regardless of your personality, circumstances, or sensitivity level, you can take steps to minimize both your exposure to chronic stress and its negative effects on you. Stress-blocking armor does exist! And you don't have to pay a fortune or sell your soul to get it.

Causes Of Stress

What *doesn't* cause stress? Seriously, certain scenarios just seem to give rise to bad stress. Lack of sleep, poor nutrition (overeating, under-eating, or having Twinkies and Coke for breakfast), lack of exercise, too much exercise, abuse of any kind (including verbal and emotional), too much work and not enough play, financial worries, low self-esteem, depression, relationship problems—collectively or individually, these create stress in your life, especially if you keep it up (or put up with it) for an extended period of time.

Hold up your mirror—what's causing stress in your life? Take this quiz to find out. Circle the number that most closely fits your answer, and try to go with your first impression. Here's how the scoring system works: 5 is "Always," 4 is "Most of the time," 3 is "Sometimes," 2 is

"Rarely," and 1 is "Never." At the end, tally your scores to see where you are on the "stress meter."

1. In my home there's a sense of harmony and balance.	5 4 3 2 1
2. At work (or school), I feel that I'm listened to and appreciated.	5 4 3 2 1
3. I feel that things are going well in my primary relationships.	5 4 3 2 1
4. I have enough money for my (and my family's) basic needs.	5 4 3 2 1
5. My time is spent wisely.	5 4 3 2 1
6. I enjoy the work (or studies) that I do.	5 4 3 2 1
7. There are people in my life whom I really enjoy being with.	5 4 3 2 1
8. I eat a balanced diet that's delicious and mostly good for me.	5 4 3 2 1
9. I have time each week for at least some activities I like.	5 4 3 2 1
10. I get a decent amount of exercise almost every week.	5 4 3 2 1
11. The air I breathe is clean.	5 4 3 2 1
12. The water I drink is pure and refreshing.	5 4 3 2 1
13. I enjoy a good movie or a good book now and then.	5 4 3 2 1
14. My commute to work (or school) is not too bad.	5 4 3 2 1

15. I laugh out loud every day.	5 4 3 2 1
16. Overall, I like my neighborhood and the area where I live.	5 4 3 2 1
17. I get along with most of my relatives.	5 4 3 2 1
18. There's a place I can go to for some peace and quiet.	5 4 3 2 1
19. I'm not one to lose or break things, typically.	5 4 3 2 1
20. I'm not too worried about my future.	5 4 3 2 1

All right, add up your points and check your score against the following table:

If Your Score Is ...	Then You Are ...	And You Need To ...
Between 90 and 100	An enlightened guru	Share your "stress-free" life secrets with the rest of us!
Between 70 and 89	A "glass half full" kind of person	Keep doing what you're doing, and learn a few relaxation techniques
Between 55 and 69	In the middle of the road	Work on the areas of your life that call for stress reduction
Between 30 and 54	Needing some adjustments	Make improvements – learn and use stress-busting techniques
Less than 30	Stressed to the max	No getting around it – take a vacation, NOW!

Go back and take a closer look at your answers. In which areas of your life did you give yourself a 4 or a 5? In these areas, you can bet that good stressors far outweigh bad stressors. In which areas did you give yourself a 3? There's definitely room for improvement here. What steps can you take to reduce stress and inch closer to a "4" in these areas?

Where did you give yourself a 2 or a 1? Definitely focus on improving these areas of your life. You're experiencing way too much stress in these segments, and it's taking the fun out of everything. Don't let stress do that to you; take back your life!

What Are Your Stress Factors?

Next take a look at specific factors that might be contributing to excessive, chronic stress—and the discontentment that ensues—in your life. Look over the list, and check any that apply:

❏ Long commutes, being stuck in traffic, dealing with bad drivers

❏ Working too many hours, falling behind at work, too many deadlines

❏ Noisy work/school environment, hectic workplace atmosphere

❏ Friction with co-workers, peers, bosses, teachers, employees, students

❏ Too much to do, no time to enjoy leisure pursuits

❏ Tense relationships at home, arguing or not speaking

❏ Close family members/friends in trouble, ill, not doing well

❏ Noisy/frenzied home environment, no peace and quiet

❏ Financial hardships, unemployment, debt, lack of insurance

❏ Pollution, poor air/water quality, noisy/dirty environment

❏ School pressure: tests, grades, homework, huge projects, peer pressure

❏ Annoying neighbors, vandalism, loud music, unkempt surroundings

❏ Crowded stores, rising cost of living, high prices, low-quality products

❏ Personal illness, injury, health issue, pending surgery/procedure

❏ Transition: moving, divorce, marriage, death, new baby, off to college

❏ Being alone, not knowing anyone in the area, seeking love/ friendship

❏ Uncertainty: in between jobs, relationships, careers, midlife crisis

❏ Maintenance/repair: housework, broken appliances, car repairs

❏ Abuse: verbal, physical, emotional, other

❏ Alcohol, drugs, overeating, other addictions

❏ Lack of sleep, always tired, never feeling rested

❏ Too many people depend on you; people won't leave you alone

❏ Media: local news, global situation, crime, sensational news

❏ Expectations: yours, others', unrealistic, too many demands

❏ Feeling stuck in life, unhappy, depressed, lacking hope or inspiration

❑ Adjustment: new job, relationship, responsibilities, home, location

❑ Other_____

Now that you have a better idea of which stress factors in particular push your buttons, take a look at how these factors affect your daily life.

Impact Of Stress On Your Daily Life

Stress is like a giant thumb holding you down. You feel like you're struggling and working hard to get free, but you just can't get out. Try doing this day in and day out, and watch how it affects you. Excessive, prolonged stress can:

- Make you grumpy, crabby, short-tempered, and not fun to be around

- Bring you down, get you depressed, bring you to tears

- Alter your mood, demeanor, even your personality

- Cause you to lose your perspective, knock you off balance

- Create aches and pains in different parts of your body

- Trigger disease—physical, mental, emotional, or spiritual

- Prevent you from getting the rest and relaxation you need

- Make you feel sick, whether or not you are

- Cause you to snap or be mean towards people around you

- Distort or cloud your thinking

- Cause you to lose sleep or to worry too much

- Make you forget things, like places you need to be, or meetings you should attend

- Trigger excessive weight loss or weight gain

- Compromise your immune system

- Ruin your day!

Doesn't sound fun, does it? But guess what? It doesn't have to be this way! Your first step is to recognize that stress is sabotaging you, preventing the real you from expressing itself freely. The next step is to look in the mirror (figuratively speaking) and decipher which aspects of your life are being affected. You're doing good so far! Now take one more step—this time, to learn how to manage and minimize stress. Doing so will empower you by bringing greater stability, more balance, and a better perspective back into your life.

Make Stress Your Friend!

Say what? You read correctly—befriend stress. You *can* make changes so that stress works for you, not against you, just as a true friend respects your personal boundaries and knows not to cross the line. Keep stress at bay; don't let it cross the line.

Relax. It's amazing how something as simple as sitting in a tub of warm water can melt the stress away! Add a little scented natural bubble bath, and you've got a full spa experience in the privacy and convenience of your own home. No time for a bath? Then linger a few moments in the shower, feeling the hot water soothe your muscles, and wash away your stress. Other excellent relaxation techniques include meditation, yoga, tai chi, and massage. You can easily do self-massage, such as rubbing your temples in a circular fashion to relieve headaches, or rubbing your feet to make them feel better after you've been standing all day. Also to relax, try reading a good book or listening to calming music.

Move your body. When you move your body, you get your circulation going, you exercise your muscles, and you release endorphins, those wonderful "happy" chemicals. All of this is good for you! Moving your body can be as simple as getting up every twenty minutes or so to stretch. Or it can be as fun as dancing, swimming, or being part of a recreational sports team. It can be as accessible as going for a walk in your neighborhood. You choose how you move. The main thing is that you get up and move your body to shake that stress away.

Take care of yourself. You must take care of yourself. If you won't, who will? The responsibility is yours. If you're in a dangerous situation, find a safe place to go to. If there are too many demands on you and your time, learn to say no. If you're addicted to harmful substances or behaviors, get professional help. It's not selfish to take care of yourself. It's smart.

Adjust your attitude. Your body doesn't know the difference between a real and a perceived stressor; either way, it reacts just the same. So one way to reduce the effects of stress on your body is to adjust your attitude by changing the way you perceive stress. Look at a new job not as a scary prospect, but as an exciting opportunity. Your long commute to work may not be as stressful if you listen to a good book on tape during the drive. If your child gets a C on a test, it's not the end of the world; it's a chance to talk, reassure, and maybe offer a little tutoring. Change your attitude, and you'll minimize stress's hold on your life.

Breathe. The quickest, most immediate way to reduce your stress level is through deep breathing. It's available to you anywhere, it's easily accessible, and it's completely free. If you're about to meet the company president, or your future in-laws, don't stress out. Instead, take three or four slow, deep breaths. You'll be amazed at how quickly this calms you down.

Affirm yourself. Don't wait for somebody else to praise you. Affirm yourself. If you feel you did a good job, tell yourself, either silently or out loud. Did you handle a difficult situation well? Make someone feel better? Solve a problem creatively? Congratulate yourself! This will boost your self-esteem and make you more resistant to the wear and tear of daily stress. You can also read inspiring books chock full of affirmations and positive messages.

Laugh. Good humor does wonders for your psyche. It helps put things into perspective and keeps you from "sweating the small stuff." When you're reading the paper, reach for the comics. Laugh with your friends and family. Read funny books, like those written by Dave Barry, Bill Cosby, or the late Erma Bombeck. When it comes to curing stress-related ailments, laughter is by far one of the best medicines. It's an effective *and* fun stress-buster.

Conclusion

Stress may be here to stay, but you don't have to let it get the best of you. Taking pro-active, simple measures takes the bite off stress. Even if you're the busiest person in the world, you can fit in stress-free moments to give yourself a chance to recover from the stressors that bombard you. You can relieve stress while you take your shower, by taking short breaks throughout the day to stretch, even while you drive to work by listening to an entertaining or soothing tape.

You can manage stress by practicing deep breathing, which can be done anytime, anywhere, and by taking a few moments here and there to read something really funny. You can eliminate certain stressors altogether by changing harmful habits, getting professional help as needed. By making minor adjustments, one step at a time, you can beat stress before it beats you. Then you can take an honest look in the mirror and see a happier, more tranquil, better balanced YOU. Take control and create a less stressful, more enjoyable life—it's good for you, in so many ways.

Recommended Reading

The Little Book Of Stress Relief by David Posen

Stress Relief And Relaxation Techniques by Judith Lazarus

Stress Free For Good: 10 Scientifically Proven Life Skills For Health And Happiness by Frederic Luskin

The Relaxation And Stress Reduction Workbook by Martha Davis

Getting Things Done: The Art Of Stress-Free Productivity by David Allen

Serious Laughter: Live A Happier, Healthier, More Productive Life by Yvonne Conte

The Laughter Factor by Dan Keller

Dream It Do It: Inspiring Stories of Dreams Come True by Sharon Cook

365 Prescriptions For The Soul: Daily Messages Of Inspiration, Hope, And Love by Bernie Siegel

Motivation That Works: How To Get Motivated And Stay Motivated by Zev Saftlas

ABOUT THE AUTHOR

MARDI ALLEN

Mardi Allen, a Certified Life Coach and Women's Wellness Expert, is passionate about motivating and coaching women to consistently achieve life-changing results and to reach their full potential. She inspires others to create a healthy lifestyle by embracing their own power and breaking self-imposed limitations.

As the founder and president of Allen Coaching & Training, specializing in personal and professional development, Mardi's goal is to empower others to enhance their own excellence through workshops, seminars, corporate training, and one-on-one coaching.

As a business leader, entrepreneur, trainer, consultant, and professional life coach, Mardi has been involved in the training and development of thousands of employees. She has been instrumental in implementing programs in self-esteem, stress management, customer service, professional image, and time management for numerous companies. Some of her most popular seminars are Self-Empowerment, Assertiveness, Emotional Wellness, Managing Your Ideal Weight, and The Law of Attraction.

As a Life Coach specializing in Women's Wellness and Weight Management, Mardi has coached and motivated hundreds of women to attain their ideal weight and taught them the tools to maintain healthy lifestyles. Mardi will be publishing her own book about overcoming weight issues by changing one's mindset.

Mardi is a Certified Development Trainer with the Professional Woman's Network and will also be co-authoring *Women's Journey to Wellness: Mind, Body and Spirit* and *Developing Inner Beauty*. She is a frequent guest on *The Word* radio station in Dallas Texas, discussing the importance of making the right choices for a healthy lifestyle.

Mardi's life journey and personal path have been instrumental in helping others be the best they can be. Her extensive background in human behavior, management, and coaching is the foundation for her success.

Contact
Mardi Allen
Allen Training & Coaching, ACT
(214) 649-1320
coachmardi@hotmail.com
www.coachmardi.net

TWENTY-THREE

MAINTAINING A HEALTHY LIFESTYLE

By Mardi Allen

Get ready. This information is going to change your life. You are going to learn *the* key to maintaining a healthy lifestyle. With some simple tools, you'll be on your way!

Exercise 1

What do you think is the most important key to maintaining a healthy lifestyle? Before you read on, please pause for a minute; really give that question some thought; and write your answer down. You can have only one answer, so think about it.

As a life coach and motivational speaker, I am often asked this question. Once someone new finds out what I do, they want to know the one tip I can offer for maintaining a healthy, happy lifestyle.

My answer is always the same: "Self-care." I know it seems so simple, and yet we make it so hard. In working with hundreds of women, I've observed that, regardless of the situation, invariably the first thing they give up is self-care. For example, when I was in the weight-loss industry, it never failed: Whenever clients had a challenge, be it family, financial, health, or what-have-you, they quickly gave up self-care in deference to others.

Exercise 2

Think about your own situation: How much self-care do you have, and how often is it forfeited for the care of others? Take a moment and write down examples of things you have done for yourself—self-care—during the last week. If you can't think of anything, do not feel bad. Hopefully that will change after you read this chapter.

Many women feel like they must do everything, and take care of everybody. They are willing to compromise their own time and efforts for the sake of others. Unfortunately, women cannot give away what they do not have. Women cannot take care of others effectively if they don't take care of themselves.

Your Emotional Bank Account

Look at it another way; consider the typical bank account. Now think about your emotional energy being in an account. If you are constantly making withdrawals from this account, with no corresponding deposits, of course you will run out of energy. Eventually, you'll be emotionally and energetically bankrupt. That's not a place you want to be.

Emotional Bankruptcy

This is a significant problem in our society. The symptoms are everywhere: Binge eating, 67% of the population is overweight or obese, anti-depressant prescriptions are at record levels. There is increased anxiety, trouble sleeping, physical pain, and just plain old burnout. We are a society on edge; a society emotionally spent.

This affects all aspects of our well-being. Heart disease is now the number one killer of women. Stress-related illness such as heart problems, high blood pressure, migraine headaches, and ulcers cost businesses in the US more than $150-billion each year. We are tired and stressed out, and we do not have the energy to deal with major challenges that may arise in our lives.

Guilt-Free Diet

So why do women have difficulty taking time for self-care? The number one reason is guilt. Women feel guilty for looking after themselves. Women have traditionally been raised to believe that "me" time is selfish time. Many women are people-pleasers, and everyone else comes first, leaving no time for self-care. Like a paradigm shift, this sort of thinking has to change. It is not selfish to take care of *you*. Quite the contrary; by taking care of yourself, you have the emotional strength to handle the other challenges that life may toss your way.

One idea I want you to walk away with after reading this chapter is: Guilt serves no one. It is a wasted emotion. Let that settle in for a moment: Guilt is a wasted emotion. It expends large amounts of very valuable energy. Guilt serves no purpose, so let it go. It is wasted energy, and no one gets anything from it. From this point forward, put yourself on a guilt-free diet!

Before we get to solutions, consider the registers below.

Wellness Register 1

Date	Transaction Description	Deposit	Withdrawal	Wellness Balance
1-Jun	12 hr wk day, only got: 4 hrs sleep		100	-100
2-Jun	11 hr wk day, huge fight with husband		100	-200
3-Jun	purchased new vehicle, skipped 2 meals		200	-400
4-Jun	took care of sick parents, ate junk food		200	-600
5-Jun	volunteer wk all day, 5 hr wk from home		100	-700
6-Jun	10 hr wk day, problem w/new car		100	-800
7-Jun	lost job, had 4 glasses of wine, pigged out		600	-1400

Wellness Register 1: As you can see, this register has constant withdrawals, and as more and more withdrawals are made, the emotional energy debt gets deeper and deeper. Most readers have probably experienced this situation more than once in their lives. Should this account continue to be overextended and overdrawn, the accountholder will literally become emotionally bankrupt, incapable of handling the day-to-day challenges that come her way, let alone a major catastrophe.

Wellness Register 2

Date	Transaction Description	Deposit	Withdrawal	Wellness Balance
1-Jun	10 min self-care, ate 5 sm healthy meals	100	0	100
1-Jun	12 hr wk day, no sleep the night before		100	0
2-Jun	day off, got 8 hours sleep, 1 hour exercise	100	0	100
3-Jun	20 min prayer/meditation, 45 min walk	100	0	200
3-Jun	10 hr wk day, purchased new car		200	0
4-Jun	15 min affirmations in car, 64 oz water	100	0	100
4-Jun	9hr wk day, problem w/new car		100	0
5-Jun	lost job, called friend for support	100	600	-500

With Wellness Register 2 you can see that the accountholder has balanced her daily life with some self-care to counter the daily stresses of life. She is doing enough to counter the daily stresses and she is not in the hole as badly as in Register 1, if something major happens. She is still in the hole, but somewhat better equipped to deal.

Wellness Register 3

Date	Transaction Description	Deposit	Withdrawal	Wellness Balance
1-Jun	1/2 hour self care, 5 sm healthy meals	100	0	100
2-Jun	worked out 1 hr, affirmations in car	100	0	200
3-Jun	1hr coaching session, 8 oz water	200	0	400
4-Jun	1/2 hr prayer and meditation, 8 hr sleep	100	0	500
5-Jun	took a nap, went to the park 3 mile walk	100	0	600
6-Jun	rest all day and get ready to go back to wk	100	0	700
7-Jun	lost job, went to support group @ church	100	-500	300

Finally, the third Wellness Register shows a proactive and well-funded account. It shows a credit able to deal with life's unexpected challenges with grace and balance. Clearly, this woman recognizes the importance of taking care of herself.

The Wellness Wheel of Life

So, how do we get from the first to the third register? How do we overcome the dilemma of balancing the stress of work and family and still maintain a healthy lifestyle? The answer is "self-care." Start by putting some of the focus and attention on you. Stop putting yourself last and start making yourself first.

Self-care is the center of being balanced. With self-care at the core, everything else can be kept in balance. When you are rested and taking care of yourself, you are better equipped to deal with and balance the stresses of daily life. Balance creates more energy for career, friends, family, and even fun.

©mardi allen,2006

Working on your self-care will give you more energy, and provide emotional well being for eating well and maintaining a healthy weight. Self-care will allow you to nurture yourself with things other than food, so there will be less emotional eating. Ultimately, you will have more energy to work out at least five times a week, and take care of your physical body. You will be less stressed, so you will sleep better and awaken more refreshed. You will live authentically, and be comfortable with who you are.

With vibrant self-care, you can love what you're doing and do well in your career. Healthy relationships will blossom as a result of taking care of yourself. By taking care of yourself, you'll soon have fewer addictions, be they food, tobacco, or whatever. You will have more time for friends and family. Finances will fall into place, which will allow you to recognize the importance of giving.

Every aspect of the Wheel of Life is improved upon when self-care is at the core. You will have more time and energy for self-development and investing in yourself, which is the best investment you will ever make. It will allow you to become better organized, develop support networks, and set boundaries.

Five Minutes a Day – "Me Time"

I know what you are thinking: I do not have time for myself. Well, let me show you how to make *you* a priority. Initially, commit just five minutes a day to self-care. With just five minutes a day, you will see improvement in your life. The key is consistency. Habits are made with consistency. If you can give yourself time – even five minutes a day – for forty days, you can create a habit. Make the commitment. Give yourself permission to take five minutes a day for yourself.

It is five minutes a day! There are 1440 minutes in a day. True, some of those minutes are spent sleeping, eating, working, etc., but we're talking about just five minutes in a 24-hour period. I challenge all readers to come up with just five minutes in the day to devote as "Me Time." After you have created the habit of self-care, you can expand on your initial five minutes a day.

Think of it this way: If you knew that those five minutes would help to make you happier, have more inner peace, handle stress better, and have a more balanced life, would you not commit to those five minutes? We can not give away what we do not have. We can not effectively take care of someone if we are not taking care of ourselves.

So, how do we take care of ourselves? What do we do for self-care? How do we put a positive balance in that emotional account? Self-care is down time. It's alone time; a time to be quiet and listen; a time to feed your mind with power and positive thoughts. Here are some tools to use.

Prayer and Mediation

I think of prayer as talking and mediation as listening to God. We need to get quiet and listen to ourselves and to God. So often we pray and pray, but things are so chaotic that we cannot hear the answer. Once you have said your prayers, believe that they will be answered, and then listen.

Journal

What better way to get your thoughts out than to write them in a journal. It is a great way to vent without affecting others. Journaling is a great way to ask yourself mindful questions, practice gratitude and forgiveness, and great for goal setting.

Live in Gratitude

We can only hold one thought at a time, and when I am feeling sorry for myself, I immediately move into gratitude. Be grateful for where you are. That does not mean you do not want to change or improve; it just means be happy with where you are now. Write down five things that you are grateful for before you go to bed each night. It does not have to be a new house or car; it can be glasses or soap. Think of how many people in the world do not even have soap. Be grateful.

Forgiveness

Forgive yourself and forgive others. People often forget to forgive themselves. We can be especially hard on ourselves. Let it go; forgive yourself. Forgive others; not for them, but for you. If someone has done something terrible to you, forgiving them does not condone what they did; it releases you from the power they have exercised over you. Forgiveness can literally change your life.

Affirm

Affirmations are powerful tools. Affirm when you wake in the morning. Do not let negative thoughts take control of your day. You control your mind; you control your thinking. Fill your mind with positive, life-affirming thoughts.

Visualize

I absolutely love the book "The Power of Positive Thinking." It is a must-read for all of my clients. Visualization is very powerful. Spend five minutes a day visualizing what you want to materialize in your life. Believe it, then you will see it.

Making Deposits in Your Emotional Account

Remember to take those five minutes a day for yourself. You will see a difference in how you feel about yourself, and you will see your confidence and self-esteem rise to new heights. You will begin to believe in yourself, and then believe in others! In addition to taking those five minutes, you might also consider any one or more of these activities:

1. Take a nap.

2. Go to a movie.

3. Get a massage.

4. Listen to relaxing music.

5. Get a pedicure and/or a manicure.

6. Sing.

7. Celebrate your successes.

8. Take a long bath in aromatherapy.

You now have the tools necessary to achieve a healthy lifestyle. It may not seem difficult, and for some, it won't be difficult. On the other hand, some – in all honesty, many – will struggle. Just remember to take it one day at a time. Don't think about trying to get five minutes a day for yourself over the next forty days. Instead, *today* think about getting five minutes for yourself, and do it. Don't worry about tomorrow or next week. Tomorrow, do the same thing. The next day.... Well, you get the idea. Break it down into manageable bits. It is one day where you have to find five minutes; it's not a forty-day program. Take it one day at a time, and in no time at all, forty days will have come and gone. You'll be amazed at the results.

It is important to never leave the scene of a self-help book without an action plan, so here is your action plan. Fill out the blank "Wellness Registry" with at least three things you can do in the next week for "Me Time." Start making deposits in your emotional wellbeing account today, and start making self-care the center of your Wellness Wheel of Life.

Blank Register

Date	Transaction Description	Deposit	Withdrawal	Wellness Balance

TAKE CARE OF YOU

One of my favorite quotes is from the movie *Pretty Woman*, "Take care of you!" I love saying it, and I try to end all correspondence with it. You deserve to live your best life now, filled with good health, love, prosperity, and inner-peace. And remember, take care of you!

Notes:

ABOUT THE AUTHOR

PHYLLIS S. QUINLAN

Phyllis S. Quinlan currently residents in Flushing, New York. She has over 30 years experience in the healthcare industry with 25 years at a management level in both acute and long term care settings. She is presently pursuing her Doctorate Degree in Healthcare Administration at the Kennedy-Western University.

Phyllis is the president of MFW Consultants To Professionals, a consulting firm serving the educational, personal coaching, and managerial needs of individuals and organizations. As a certified legal nurse consult, she also serves as an expert witness to many attorney-clients.

Phyllis' article entitled, "Capitalize on a Hidden Treasure" was published in the October 2001 New York edition of *NursingSpectrum*. Phyllis is a contributing author for PWN and a member of the PWN International Speakers Bureau and is available internationally to assist the individual client or organization with professional development needs.

Phyllis' most cherished role is that of godmother to five fabulous young women. She wants to thank her mother, Madeline Walsh Quinlan, for all her support and encouragement and dedicates this chapter to her.

Contact
Phyllis Quinlan, RNC, MS, CEN CCRN, CLNC
MFW Consultants To Professionals, Inc
147-20 35th Avenue #2B
Flushing, New York 11354
718 661 4981
mfwconsultants@mindspring.com

TWENTY-FOUR

CHASING THE ILLUSION OF PERFECTION

By Phyllis S. Quinlan, RNC, MS

There are very few adult women who would openly admit that the yardstick by which they use to measure themselves is one that is determined and held by others. Yet, our actions reveal something very different. The media constantly puts forth imagines of what others consider to be beautiful, accomplished, bright, sexy, a good parent, the new 40, and even happy women. We seem compelled to take in this information. It is like a quick glance into a mirror to ensure that we look OK. What are we thinking? A standard set by others is like a mirage. It is an illusion you can never attain.

Perfectionism in the positive sense is known as *Intrinsically Motivated Perfectionism*. It is a quest for excellence. Intrinsic motivation can lead to outstanding accomplishments. However, perfectionism in the negative sense is known as *Extrinsically Motivated Perfectionism*. This form of perfectionism tends to be disabling. It is a belief that one is worthless in the eyes of others unless one can present oneself and one's work perfectly. It is vital to understand which type of motivation is fueling your behavior.

Chasing the Illusion: A Price Too Dear To Pay

The whole notion of perfection insinuates that some individuals are perfect and some are not. There is a high price for chasing this or any illusion. At the very least, we are flirting with disillusionment. On a personal level, the price can include loosing peace of mind, compromised health, failed relationships, and perhaps inevitable failure.

One approaches the danger zone when the intrinsic pursuit for accomplishment is replaced by a need to maintain an extrinsic image. The balance shifts. The achievement of being a so-called superwoman is no longer personal; it becomes business. As you work to maintain the image, the stress and fatigue builds until it is a constant state of being. You may sense the need to make a modification, but you are uncertain of where to cut back. You find yourself chanting a new mantra, "The image must not suffer." You do not have the illusion; it has you. The irony is that those of us passionately chasing extrinsic perfection are unknowingly sending a message that we have a challenged self-esteem. Whatever the cost, it is much too high, and a very unnecessary line item on our psychological budget.

Reality Check

It is no illusion that many women must do things twice as well as a man in the same position just to be seen as equal. However, I am more troubled about the illusions created by woman that are targeted primarily at woman. Professional nurses have been caught up in this chase, and I am no exception. I am not certain when the moment came. Perhaps it was because the change was subtle. For most of my early adult life I struggled to ensure that I would be seen as equal and be afforded equal opportunities. Indeed, I am a child of the fifties with my most formative years shaped by the woman's movement. However, there came a time when being seen as equal was no longer good enough. The new benchmark was to be seen as perfect, a superwoman.

I entered into the nursing profession in the seventies, when its core knowledge base demanded the incorporation of academic preparation as a fundamental. Associate programs gave way to baccalaureate programs. Graduate programs evolved. Clinical Specialists were replaced by Nurse Practitioner. But, the finish line was elusive. Clinical certification in a chosen specialty was the newest benchmark. More than one certification couldn't hurt. The time when student nurses strived to complete a hospital affiliated training program was in the distant past. I bought into this pursuit of excellence whole-heartedly. I encouraged my friends, my family, and my colleagues to do so as well. In the beginning, I viewed this as growing pains vital to the development of a profession. But now I must ask, are we more credible and competent, or are we just incredibly credentialed?

Opinions on what it took to be a competent nurse divided the profession into opposing camps. It was not long before this professional growth process turned malignant. Healthy dialogue on the vision of the profession for the twenty-first century was replaced by destructive, judgmental attitudes of right and wrong. We sent the message to many that they were not good enough, instead of standing together and lobbying for educational funding that would support each nurse in attaining an accepted standard of preparation. We perpetuated the image of women undermining women. There is a global shortage of nurses today. In chasing this illusion we are faced with that reality. There are many reasons sited for this global shortage, but it is time to now ask, did we become a part of our own problem? Clearly, the field of nursing is not alone in moving the finish line. I have heard similar concerns voiced by women who have chosen teaching, law, or homemaking as their profession. So, is this being done to us or are we, as woman, doing it to ourselves? My feminist self cannot help but point out that I know of few men caught in this dilemma.

There is no doubt that the price on a professional level can be dearer because it is a blow to us all. We confuse style with substance. We do not remain open and supportive. We judge and condescend. Can we move to a place where we respect differences without attaching a value of better or worse to it? It is my professional hope that we can. But sadly, I've witnessed the same destructive attitudes appearing in every generation of nurses after mine. It moves me to tears to hear young nurses say that things will get better when more men are attracted to the profession. Unfortunately, it seems the more we organize, the more we polarize.

So where do we begin? Why not start with ourselves? We can let go of our personal chase and commit to become a superwoman in support of a least one other woman. We can each personally resolve to stop this cannibalistic behavior in ourselves and lead by example. I believe change can happen, one person at a time. It must. We have come a long way, but unless we end the undermining of each other, we will be perpetuating the illusion instead of creating a new, stronger reality. The perfection we chase, and should encourage other women to chase, must be intrinsically motivated if we are to succeed.

So how does one maintain an intrinsic drive for achievement and not allow extrinsic motivations to influence your life? Consider these suggestions:

- Think your way through the challenges in your life. Feeling your way though the challenges can be very subjective. Viewing an issue subjectively can cause tunnel vision and limit your ability to problem-solve. Approaching a challenge with an objective viewpoint allows you to open your peripheral vision and see all the options that may lead to the best decision.

- Be mindful of why you are taking on a new project or making a big change. Question your motives. Is your motivation intrinsically or extrinsically driven? It is a simple reality check that can help you identify potential conflicts early.

- Resist the temptation to say yes to everyone and anything. Saying no is not the same as saying I can't. Saying no is saying that my responsibility is to complete what I have already committed to before I take on more.

- Trust and delegate. Realize that successful delegation is achieved by delegating timely, delegating to an appropriate person, and touching base periodically to ensure mutual understanding of the desired outcome and deadline.

- Learn how to do task segmentation. Breaking down projects makes it easier to wrap your mind around them. It is essential to setting priorities and keeping them in perspective.

- Do not allow your work ethic to be used against you. Finding yourself in the role of the "go-to person" on a constant base is not a complement. The added stress can deplete you of your energy and sow the seeds of frustration in relationships. When you sense that individuals or members of the team are not contributing equally, set appropriate limits. Resist efforts to place you in the role of the enabler.

- There can be no achievement without a focused mind. Practice being quiet. Listen to the wisdom that can come to you in a quiet moment.

- Women are gifted with intuition. Work to develop your intuitive self by respecting that inner voice that can guide you. However, it is vital to remember that intuition is a knowing, not a feeling.

- Remember, professionals do not become overwhelmed. Professionals reconsider, reorganize and reprioritize.

Being Equal to the Task of Life

Understand and accept that the development of your inner self, and not your outer image, is one of the true tasks of this life. This is your first step. Work to know yourself. Embrace your strengths and acknowledge your shortcomings. Find the humor in your own physical and emotional challenges. Accept all that you can about yourself, and then set achievable goals on improving the rest. This process cannot work unless the goals you set are yours and yours alone. Walk your personal and professional path with courage and integrity. When you can look in the mirror and see a friend, not a challenge or a contest, you will have made a good start.

Exercise 1

List three goals that you have set for yourself and identify your motivation to achieve these goals as intrinsic or extrinsic.

A. _____   ❏ Intrinsic   ❏ Extrinsic

B. _____   ❏ Intrinsic   ❏ Extrinsic

C. _____   ❏ Intrinsic   ❏ Extrinsic

For each goal identified as extrinsically motivated, take a moment to reflect on the issues behind your decision.

Exercise 2

List one major project you are currently involved with or will soon be starting. Now break this project down into at least 5 segments and assign a date of completion to each segment.

Project: _____

Segment A._____ Date of Completion_____

Segment B._____ Date of Completion_____

Segment C. _____ Date of Completion_____

Segment D. _____ Date of Completion_____

Segment E._____ Date of Completion_____

Exercise 3

Reflect on the last time you felt or stated that you were overwhelmed. Now identify how you could have reconsidered, reorganized and reprioritized your responsibilities at that time so that the situation was more manageable.

_____

_____

_____

Reference

1. pages.mhlearningnetwork.com/jdelisle/id25.html

ABOUT THE AUTHOR

KARYN E. TAYLOR

Karyn E. Taylor is President and founder of The Whole Self Design Consulting Group, which is dedicated to inspiring and motivating growth in individuals and organizations through seminars, training, workshops, consulting, and coaching.

She is a member of the Professional Woman Network (PWN) and is a certified trainer in Diversity and Women's Issues, Professional Presentation Skills, and Career Coaching through the PWN.

Karyn's expertise in the areas of Diversity, Leadership, and Career and Success Coaching has given her the opportunity to empower and enrich the lives of others at work, at church and in her community. Ms. Taylor is a member of the Pittsburgh Human Resources Association, Toastmasters International; she is also a volunteer Victim/Offender Mediator with the Pittsburgh Mediation Center.

Ms. Taylor completed her Bachelors of Arts Degree in Legal Studies at the University of Pittsburgh and her Master of Arts Degree in Industrial and Labor Relations at Indiana University of Pennsylvania. She has an extensive background in Human Services, Human Resources and Training.

Karyn would like to thank her mother and mentor Dr. Elayne Arrington, for all of her support, guidance and inspiration. Linda Ellis Eastman, President of PWN, and Alicia Smith of Alicia Smith Consulting and Training, LLC are also Karyn Taylor's mentors. She acknowledges the contributions of Janice Myers and Aldine Coleman to this project.

Contact
Karyn E. Taylor
The Nuin Center
5655 Bryant Street
Pittsburgh, PA 15206
www.nuincenter.com
(412) 235-1739
(888) 609-8992

TWENTY-FIVE

TAKE OFF THE MASK! RELEASE YOUR AUTHENTIC SELF

By Karyn Elayne Taylor

Masks serve people in many ways. They allow us to encounter our fears with some measure of courage and safety. As adults, we are masters at creating masks that are either invisible or transparent to the outside world, and sometimes to ourselves. The mask is created for those from whom we think that we have something to hide. Unfortunately, many people feel that they have nothing to offer or "bring to the table" as themselves, for others to "see". Masking is what we use when we choose to role-play. This is not your authentic self; it is the substitution for your true person, who, in your own perception, is better prepared to face the world. What motivates a person to wear a mask? Our motivations can come from many sources, including our feelings of inadequacy, lack of self-worth or self-esteem, or inability to deal with the present situation.

Most of us learned the concept of "masking" as children. We wore masks as a game, to try to fool people into thinking that we were someone else—some fictional or fantasy person or thing whose characteristics exceeded anything that a "regular" human being could ever accomplish or achieve. Of course, we soon learned that, no matter how exceptional our characters were, in the end, we had to take off the masks and return to our authentic selves.

Some people surmise that, in order to pursue our dreams until they become realities, it is necessary for us to "fake it until we make it", "fit in where we can get in", or "do as the Romans do" (when in Rome). The problem with this type of thinking is that, if we "fake it", when will our "real" selves emerge? And if we "fit in", how or when will we recognize that in life, "one size does *not* fit all"? Or, if we "do as the Romans do", when will *our* desires and dreams come to fruition? Each of us must therefore ask herself these questions—who is my authentic self, what do I really want out of life, and why is it such a struggle to pursue my goals and personal needs without the burden of guilt? One reason could be that many of us have received, over time, very loving familial and cultural messages that have told us to "take care of others' needs" first. As a result, we find it difficult to make our needs a matter of top priority. It is only now, in this time of self-improvement, that we are willing and able to focus on the *idea* of developing a healthy sense of self-concept.

The American Heritage College Dictionary defines self-concept as, "something formed in the mind about one's self; a thought, or notion about one's self."

What does "self-concept" mean to you?

_____

_____

_____

How has "masking" hindered your concept of yourself in the past?

_____

_____

_____

In his book, *One: The Art and Practice of Conscious Leadership*, Dr. Lance Secretan defines being "authentic" this way—"Committing ones self to showing up and being fully present in all aspects of life; removing the mask and becoming a real, vulnerable, and intimate human being - a person without self-absorption who is genuine and emotionally and spiritually connected to others."

- What does "authentic self" mean to you?

_____

_____

_____

_____

- How has masking manifested itself in your life? (e.g. lack of motivation, procrastination, pretense that you are content without pursuing your dreams)

_____

_____

_____

_____

- What improvements can you make to allow you to show your authentic self to the world?

_____

_____

_____

_____

Some of the characteristics of an authentic self can be found in the words following. Since each of our journeys differ, try creating an acrostic of your own.

Authentic Self

- ✓ **A**ssume an Attitude of Gratitude
- ✓ **U**nveil Your Purpose
- ✓ **T**ransform Your Challenges
- ✓ **H**onor Your Time
- ✓ **E**steem Yourself
- ✓ **N**urture Yourself
- ✓ **T**ake Risks
- ✓ **I**gnite Your Dreams
- ✓ **C**ommit to Your Code of Conduct
- ✓ **S**eek to Discover Yourself
- ✓ **E**liminate Your Barriers
- ✓ **L**ive with Passion
- ✓ **F**ace Your Fears

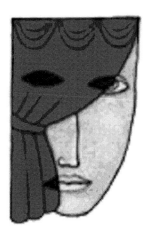

Assume an Attitude of Gratitude

As we begin to focus on our authentic selves and the natures of our purposes, we are able to see the "process" differently. Our losses become our lessons; our trials become our triumphs. Through the eyes of gratitude, the highs and the lows become less extreme. We can stand when we used to fall; situations that caused us to feel as if we had reached a "bottom" are now, through the eyes of gratitude, transformed from the bottom rung of the ladder to the first step towards possibilities!

This doesn't mean that we won't be faced with challenges; but a heart and mind that are filled with gratitude allow us not only to be "faced" with challenges, but also to "face" our challenges and press onward, toward the purpose for which we have been created.

Hearts of gratitude enhance our true selves because they remind us that all that we have comes from God.

Activity for this section

- Start a Gratitude Journal.

- Gratitude journals are great faith-enhancers and can give you much needed encouragement in times of struggle.

- Take time each day to write something for which you are grateful.

Unveil Your Purpose

When the concept of purpose is addressed, many people feel uncomfortable and unsure about the best way to approach this seemingly unfamiliar territory. You may have experienced moments of clarity about what you were "born to do" or have been "called to do"; however, those moments of clarity can become clouded by life and the living of it. You owe it to yourself to *make* time to "re-capture" those moments of clarity and to remember the following ideas:

- Purposes are shared and your purpose is unique.

- Purposes were created to meet a human need.

- Revelations are connected to your natural abilities and talents.

- Purpose acceptance is a life-long process and needs re-evaluation often.

- Purpose is unfolding within you and around you.

Transform Your Challenges

To be challenged is to have your abilities or resources tested, to declare an act or statement of defiance, to be called to engage in a competition, or to be summoned to action, effort, or use. Facing your challenges can be an excellent way to strengthen your concept of yourself. You know that everyone has challenges, and you know that some of your challenges have been super *challenging!* Successful people confront their challenges and endure through the end. Are you always successful? Not if you look at success in terms of "winning" or "losing". Remember, your life will be filled with challenges, but the way that you look at your challenges and process positive ways to handle them will determine your outcomes!

Honor Your Time

Each day we are given 24 hours of time. Most of us are able to use this time in a purposeful and productive manner. However, some of us use our lack of effective time-management skills as a way to mask ourselves from the outside world.

- If this is an area in which you need improvement, what steps would you need to take to start the process?

_____

_____

_____

_____

- If you knew that today would be your last day on Earth, what would you do differently?

  _____

  _____

  _____

  _____

- Who would you want to see?

  _____

  _____

  _____

  _____

- With whom would you wish to talk?

  _____

  _____

  _____

  _____

- Where would you want to go?

_____

_____

_____

_____

What stops you from doing these things or planning these things today? For most of us, the answer is "nothing". We have just been so busy "living" that we have not taken the time to be "alive"! The good news is, now that you have taken an honest look at the way that things have been in the past, you can begin to make improvements in this area, either alone, or with the help of an outside source. But the bottom line for you will be improving your time-management skills, which will enhance your life and increase the amount of joy that you experience while you are on this journey towards purpose and fulfillment.

Esteem Yourself

Having esteem for your true self, regarding your life with the respect that it deserves, and viewing your purpose in life with a sense of honor and high regard, will help you achieve your goals. As you learn to be kind to yourself and to treat yourself with the same love and compassion that you give to others, you will find that your new journey can be both enjoyable and enriching.

As you travel on this new journey, treat yourself to the following:

- Listen to your inner voice. (That's how this journey got started, isn't it?)

- Follow your *own* advice. (You *really* do know yourself better than anyone else.)

- Trust yourself.

- Build a relationship with the new "empowered" you.

Nurture Yourself

As you continue on your path to authenticity, remember to make time to nurture yourself. Here are some suggestions:

- Take time each week to do something that you love.

- Spend time with loved ones.

- Reward yourself for a job well done (or a well-made attempt).

- Re-energize yourself through exercise and healthy eating.

- Enjoy a good book or a movie.

- Reconnect with some old friends.

Take Risks

As we continue to discover ways to "unmask" ourselves and to become acquainted with our authentic selves, our comfort levels become elevated, and we are now ready and able to live in the fullness of our purposes, to launch out in faith, and to take some risks.

You've already embarked on the biggest risk of all, acting on your innermost dreams and desires. Now it's time to re-examine your ideas about taking risks with old and new relationships, and re-evaluating your status in these relationships. You are now able to gain new insight into your old way of thinking, and develop new ways to build trust in personal and professional relationships. With your new sense of freedom, you are no longer "stuck" in the old ways of bondage; thus you continue to grow.

Ignite Your Dreams

As with any plan of action, it is imperative that you have a good strategy and a well thought-out plan. You might want to start small with a journal or a ledger, to keep track of your progress. Seeing your progress in written form can be encouraging and motivating. You might want to meet with someone who is knowledgeable in the area of your interest. Networking of any sort can be a valuable tool for the success of your plan.

Activity for this section

- Develop a progressive action plan and chart your progress.

- Set daily, weekly, and monthly goals.

- Start with small goals and increase the depth of your goals as you progress.

Commit to Your Code of Conduct

As a commitment to yourself, create your Personal Code of Conduct! As an example, I have included mine.

My Personal Pledge of Conduct

I will commit myself to constant improvement.

I will base my accountability on honesty and integrity.

I will be dependable, trustworthy, and respectful to others.

I will observe the Golden Rule in my dealing with others.

I will communicate openly and exercise discretion in my speech.

I will continue to be a reliable and responsible person.

I will take full responsibility for how each of my days turns out.

Your Personal Code of Conduct

_____

_____

_____

_____

_____

_____

_____

_____

Sign_____

Date _____

Seek to Discover Yourself

My hope for you in this section is that you to expand your awareness. Do something different this week. Take a trip; read a book of particular interest; or telephone a school or university to get information about a particular class. Join Toastmasters, take an exercise class, or begin work on your pilot's license.

Write down some things you want to explore:

This week:

_____

_____

_____

Next week:

_____

_____

_____

All it takes is one step to open up all kinds of new possibilities for your life. Follow your heart's desire and begin something new today! You owe it to yourself; you will appreciate the new you!

Eliminate Your Barriers

Most of us have struggled with barriers at some time in our lives; many have been self-imposed. We have successfully eliminated some of these barriers and have triumphant stories to share. Some barriers, however, have been persistent or recurring, and can be a source of discomfort, discouragement, and dysfunction. In the past, our "masked" selves could disguise them with "masking" techniques, but our authentic selves will no longer allow such conditions to exist! We are now able to search our inner selves as well as outside sources for some much needed assistance. Searching our inner selves will allow us to communicate with the authentic persons that we are and honestly determine the source of our discomfort and what needs to be done to alleviate the pain. Sometimes the answer is simple; sometimes it is much more complex. Either way, we are now able to allow ourselves to do what we need in order to become healthy, well-adjusted adults.

Take time to reflect on some barriers that you have already overcome.

- Which barriers still need to be dealt with?

_____

_____

_____

_____

- What do you need to do to start the process?

  _____

  _____

  _____

  _____

- Who can support you through this process?

  _____

  _____

  _____

  _____

- What will be a successful outcome for you?

  _____

  _____

  _____

  _____

Live with Passion

"Go confidently in the direction of your dreams!
Live the life you have imagined."
— Thoreau

On a recent visit to a local bookstore, I was drawn to the stationery section. In just a few minutes, I was fascinated by the way in which this section had been enhanced, with a clear emphasis on living a passion-filled life. The cards, tablets, writing instruments, and attractive daily planners all encouraged and invited the customers to pursue the things in life that would bring them pleasure and enjoyment. I got the idea from this visit that it is important to remember to do the following:

- Live with your eyes wide open.

- Trust it or adjust it.

- Fall in love with a new idea.

- Live your life with passion and your heart will sing.

Thought for Today

Dance as though no one is watching you.
Love as though you have never been hurt before.
Sing as though no one can hear you.
Live as though Heaven is on earth. -Souza

Face Your Fears

As we release our authentic selves, we are faced with new ways of thinking, new ways of being, and new ways of walking. Some of these new paths can be paved with old thoughts, ideas, and even some memories of things that did not work out as we anticipated. In the past, fear of the unknown has hindered us from achieving our dreams and pursuing our goals. And we were not alone. Fear has held many people back from pursuing their purposes. Take a few moments and answer these questions:

- How has fear negatively impacted your life?

_____

_____

_____

_____

- What opportunities do you feel that you have missed?

_____

_____

_____

_____

- Why did you miss the opportunities?

  _____

  _____

  _____

  _____

- How can you turn these around?

  _____

  _____

  _____

  _____

- What steps can you take to reduce the negative impact of fear in your life?

  _____

  _____

  _____

  _____

- When will you take these steps?

  _____

  _____

  _____

  _____

- Has fear played a positive influence in your life? If so, please share that experience, and what made this different than the experience stated above?

  _____

  _____

  _____

  _____

There are volumes of literature verifying that fear is one of the most negative emotions that we can experience. But we do not need to focus on the literature to know that this is true. Clearly, our life experiences have shown us this. When we play it safe and are afraid to try new ways of thinking or acting, we can miss out on many experiences that will help us to achieve our dreams. See fear as the self-imposed trap that it is. Do not let fear cripple your aspirations and prevent you from becoming who you are meant to be and all you are meant to be.

You have a new resolve! You will not be dissuaded! You have come to realize that you have been created for a purpose. You have been chosen to fulfill your hearts desire. You have been waiting for a day to go forward and to be successful at being yourself! As you go forth, remember the following:

- Have an Attitude of Gratitude.

- Transform your challenges into success.

- Realize that your time is precious.

- Be good to yourself.

- Believe in yourself.

- Dream *Big* Dreams.

- Take personal responsibility.

- Expand your awareness.

- Love yourself (only you know what you *really* need).

- Eliminate your barriers.

- Measure your success by your *own* yardstick.

But most of all……

BE YOURSELF -- PERFECTLY!

Related Reading

Think & Grow Rich by Napoleon Hill

Reach Your Potential – How to Overcome Self-Defeating Behavior by Sheri O. Zampell

The Purpose Driven Life by Rick Warren

Pathways to Purpose for Women by Katie Brazelton

ABOUT THE AUTHOR

ELIZABETH M. WATERBURY, P.E., P.P., C.M.E.

Elizabeth Waterbury is the President and founder of E. M. Waterbury & Associates Consulting Engineers, a successful Consulting Engineering firm specializing in Land Use and Land Use Development. The focus of her career is to provide quality professional engineering services with a commitment to innovation and personal attention. Ms. Waterbury's firm consists of a talented group of female professionals and support staff who have made their mark in this specialized field of engineering, which is highly competitive and dominated by larger engineering firms.

When not working in her firm, Ms. Waterbury mentors others in professionalism, leadership and balance. This is accomplished through her many and diverse roles that vary from university professor to providing speeches as a member of The Professional Woman International Speakers Bureau. Her unique ability to channel her technical mind into creative and down-to-earth communication allows her to mentor to a broad range of individuals. One of her most honored rolls was to be the keynote speaker for the Southwest Regional Conference for the Society of Woman Engineer's. She has also been honored as a member of the International Advisory Board for The Professional Woman Network since 1990.

Her most cherished role is that of mother. She has worked hard since her daughter's birth to raise her daughter while running her firm. She is well versed in the difficulties that face women who wish to pursue their career, as well as be active in their family's lives. Her message of balance, defining personal success, and personal empowerment is carried through in all of her endeavors.

Contact
Elizabeth Waterbury, P.E., P.P., C.M.E.
E. M. Waterbury & Associates, P.A.
17 Monmouth Street
Red Bank, NJ 07701
(732) 747-6530
Fax (732) 747-6778
EMWAssoc@aol.com
www.protrain.net

CARING FOR AGING PARENTS

By Libby Waterbury

I would like to dedicate this chapter to my loved ones who have passed, the most recent being my father. My siblings and I have moved into the next chapter of our lives. My father was the end of the generation that was before us. As my sister said to her sons on the day Dad died, "Be nice to me as I am a 50 year old orphan." Although it was said with a little bit of dark humor at the time, there is quite a bit of truth in it, as it signified our step into being the next in line in the circle of life.

Introduction

I have spent much of the last five years being personally involved with the issues and care of the elderly. I am also a working mom. I remember the first time I heard the labeling of the "Sandwich Generation, the generation of people who are caring for the children that they had later in life, and at the same time caring for the aging family members. We are therefore "sandwiched" between the demands of both extremes of the life cycle at the same time. I guess if you add work into that mix, then I am a triple-decker. I had never considered myself in a particular category before. The use of various labeling, i.e. Baby Boomers, X Generation, Y Generation, seemed impersonal and set the individual up for the stereotyping. In this instance however, I could feel the pressure squeezing me to provide to both the young and the old at the same time. The title of "Sandwich Generation" feels like it accurately described the events going on.

What's the Secret?

I am happy to say that as a group, my siblings and I were able to pull together over the past five years and care for my uncle, my aunt, their disabled son, my mother-in-law, our father, and now my father-in-law. It was not done out of obligation, but out of love and respect for the effort given to us, even through their difficult times and recognition of the eternal value of the relationship. We all work, have our own health issues, and are responsible for our own families. My husband and I both manage our own businesses and yes, we do have an issue in our family with the "super *person* syndrome"!

Through all my experiences of caring for my elderly parents, may I offer advice on how to manage this with the least amount of stress:

1. Know Yourself - Caring for the elderly is like a reverse process of caring for your kids. Children go from needing help to independence. Our parents can go from independence to needing help.

You've heard the saying that 'children cannot properly care for children'.

Although I believe that is said mainly about young teenage pregnancies, I offer that it relates here, too. To care for elderly parents who often revert back to being children with their needs, we cannot be children ourselves anymore. We have to work through the issues (also known as "baggage") we have from our own childhoods, so that we can move beyond seeing parents or elders through the eyes of a child, and see them as human beings through our *adult* eyes.

We all carry issues from our childhood. That is natural. The important part is working through them so that they do not hinder us through our whole life, or during the process of caring for our parents. (This can be complicated if you suffered extremely negative childhood experiences, such as being abused physically, sexually, or emotionally.) We must work through those emotions and learn to forgive. We must face our elderly parents with the heart and mind of an adult, not a child.

Speaking of acting as an adult, if you are not an only child, then you also need to know your siblings. We can be in our 50's and still sound like nine or ten year–olds, when it comes to agreeing on family issues. We all have our baggage, both from our parents and our siblings. When we enter into discussions of what to do and how to do it, this baggage complicates the task. The difficult task is that we cannot change others. We can only change ourselves, and work on our own issues.

I offer however, that by changing ourselves, we also change how we relate to others, so indirectly change occurs outside of ourselves. I have seen the magic of this work within my own family. This will be very important as you jointly work together with your siblings to care for your aging parents. The team must come together.

2. You Get What You Give - If we want people to care for us, then we must care for others. If we feel that there is no room in our lives to care for those in need at this time, then that is the example we are setting for the generation that will care for us when we are in need.

3. Come to Terms With the Cycle of Life - We must accept that the aging and death process are a part of life. These are not easy issues for people to face. We try to keep our bodies fit and young looking. We use plastic surgery and chemicals to reduce the signs of aging. We try to keep up with the times with our attire and language. So in the middle of our efforts to recapture our youth and keep things on the upswing, why would we want to be faced with the reality of a perceived downswing?

I take my daughter's brownie troop and some neighborhood children to an assisted living facility to sing during the holidays. When I first started this holiday ritual, I had three children that were willing to go. The kids enjoyed it so much that they passed the word. The group has grown to over twenty kids and five adults. One of the obstacles that I have had is from the parents of interested children who were not willing to give permission to allow the children to participate. The parents would not allow the interaction because they thought it would not be healthy for the kids to see "that". I offer the idea that it is important to embrace aging as a part of life, and that we should not turn our eyes away from this important cycle.

4. The Only Thing You Can Count On Is Change – My time spent caring for the elderly and disabled in our family was very similar to when I was caring for my mother when she was chronically ill. Just when I would get into a routine and think that I have it figured out, it would change. It can take only a second for a condition to change-a stroke, a fall, or just a point where something gives in the body, due to wear and tear over the years. These are quick and can change a person's ability, either physically or mentally, for their rest of their lives, or for an extended period of recovery. Even a simple thing of not drinking enough fluids to stay hydrated, or keeping up with their diet, can change things without an easily visible warning. It was somewhat like when I would get use to my baby moving onto crawling and getting everything out of that reach, and she decided to walk. I had to redo what I was doing to additionally baby-proof everything. I knew it was coming, but somehow it always felt like the change crept up on me.

With the elderly, the same type of thing happens in reverse. When you are just thinking you have the person set in their environment, something changes and more has to be done or undone. Be prepared for the ups and downs, and to roll with the changes. It can be frustrating.

It is difficult to watch people of any age progress into stages of being less than. It takes love, patience, empathy, and stamina. I remember being at a seminar where the presenter was having us do various exercises to increase our empathy for the aging. We wore glasses that restricted our vision, did exercises that changed the way we tasted food and smelled aromas, and ones that restricted what we could do physically. It was enlightening. We were fortunate to be able to do a comparison of the two conditions side by side to get a clear sense of the difficulty.

5. Remember to Care for Yourself - This is one area where I am not always successful! Remember to eat, to drink lots of fluids, rest, and set aside some quality time. (I also need to set time aside for laughter! For me, I escape to watch a silly movie at home. I need something light. The sillier the movie, the better!

Plan for fun and self-pampering such as a massage, pedicure, or little get-away trips to see a friend. (If your elderly parent is staying at home with you, then consider hiring a companion for them while you are away for the weekend.) Remember, it is vital that you as caregiver take care of yourself!

Where Will They Live?

One of the main considerations with caring for the elderly is where they are going to live. That is a financial and logistic consideration. Having a roof over their head is just the beginning.

Stay in Their Home or Apartment Independently - The practicality of this will depend on their ability to have adequate funds to sustain this type of independent living. They must be able to obtain help as needed for the daily items listed on the checklist (at the end of this chapter). Help can be brought into the home for cleaning, meals, personal care assistance, and you name it!

In addition to at-home care, there are a couple things that will help the individual that has mobility to stay on their own a bit longer. One is the Life Alert system. The individual wears the system either on a chain around the neck, or on their wrists. In case of a fall or an emergency where they cannot get to a phone, they can press the button and help will be sent to the home. The other option is to get meals brought into the home. There is a wonderful group called "Meals on Wheels" that will provide hot meals to the individual, if they are unable to prepare food for themselves.

The problem with a stay-at-home situation is that the elder's life can become very isolated. For those that are not independent, there are

Adult Day Care facilities that are geared towards providing activities during the day, and giving the caregiver a break

Living With Family – The concerns that exist when the elderly are living on their own are similar if they are to live with family, especially if everyone in the home works outside of the house. The individual would need to be evaluated to determine to what extent they can be left on his or her own. When placing the elder in the home, it is important to be aware of the adequacy of the living conditions to suit their needs. Is there adequate space for walkers or wheel chairs? Are there stairs to maneuver? Throw rugs on the floor that could slip out from under them?

Are there bathrooms equipped with handicap bars? Be sure the home is elder-proofed and elder-equipped before having your parent move in.

Assisted Living Facilities – I am a big fan of this type of facility! A resident may enter as a person requiring almost no assistance, and then get the additional assistance as needs arise, without changing their living condition. They get meals and maintenance of their home. They can stay as independent as their needs allow. Activities are planned on and off the site throughout the day.

Nursing Homes - Nursing homes are different than Assisted Living Facilities.

There may come a time when the medical level of care that is required on a daily basis exceeds that that can be provided by Assisted Living. That is when nursing homes can be considered. Some of the Assisted Living Facilities have a nursing home component connected to the facility, but not all. Prior to admittance to any facility, a medical review would be performed by the facility to see if the needs and the facilities are a good fit.

Adult Day Care – Adult Day Care facilities provide a place where individuals can go during the day for social interaction and activities. The intention is to allow the caregiver a break. Many have transportation available that will pick up and deliver the individual from their home (or yours). I recommend that you visit any of the facilities under consideration to see if their program meets your desired level of activity for your parent. I have been to some that are more childlike in their programs, and others that appeared more adult in their offerings.

Independence Checklist

The following is a checklist for you to use as you consider whether your aging parent is capable of living on his or her own. You may wish to make several copies of this chart and refer to it as your mother or father moves from one stage (independence) to another (nursing home). The more you are "armed" with information about what your parent may need, the better you will serve their needs.

I wish you strength, courage, and an abundance of love as you care for your aging parents. Hopefully, you will have gained support from this chapter, reminding you to take good care of yourself, as the role of caregiver can be extraordinarily taxing. You and your parent deserve the best!

Independence Checklist *

Task	Independent	Needs assistance	Can not do
Mobility			
Able to stand			
Able to walk			
Transfer from one to another			
Sit down			
Climb stairs			
Drive a car			
Hand eye coordination			
Bend over			
Housekeeping			
Clean dishes			
Operate a vacuum			
Prepare foods on prescribed diet			
General living space cleaning			
Wash and fold laundry			
Operate a phone Manage and pay bills			
Track finances			
Maintain yard, if applicable			

Make bed or change sheets			
Oversee helpers, if applicable			
Grocery shopping			
Strength for carrying items			
Mental ability			
Long term memory			
Short term memory			
Ability to organize thoughts			
Ability to keep track of appointments			
Remember to shut off appliances			
Remember where they put things			
Personal care			
Able to shower or bathe			
Able to dress oneself			
Hair and teeth maintenance			
Ability to shave, where applicable			
Ability to manage medicines			
Take medications as prescribed			

Bladder control			
Bowel control			
Strong enough to stand up for oneself			
Senses function			
Eye sight			
Hearing			

* The above checklist is intended to be an aide to recognizing needs of the individual, and may not be all-inclusive. Please review with the individual's physician or an eldercare professional to determine the proper care and treatment for the individual.

THE PROFESSIONAL WOMAN NETWORK
Training and Certification on Women's Issues

 Linda Ellis Eastman, President & CEO of The Professional Woman Network, has trained and certified over two thousand individuals to start their own consulting/seminar business. Women from such countries as Brazil, Argentina, the Bahamas, Costa Rica, Bermuda, Nigeria, South Africa, Malaysia, and Mexico have attended trainings.

Topics for certification include:
• Diversity & Multiculturalism
• Women's Issues
• Women: A Journey to Wellness
• Save Our Youth
• Teen Image & Social Etiquette
• Leadership & Empowerment Skills for Youth
• Customer Service & Professionalism
• Marketing a Consulting Practice
• Professional Coaching
• Professional Presentation Skills

If you are interested in learning more about becoming certified or about starting your own consulting/seminar business contact:

The Professional Woman Network
P.O. Box 333
Prospect, KY 40059
(502) 566-9900
lindaeastman@prodigy.net
www.prowoman.net

The Professional Woman Network
Book Series

Becoming the Professional Woman
Customer Service & Professionalism for Women
Self-Esteem & Empowerment for Women
The Young Woman's Guide for Personal Success
The Christian Woman's Guide for Personal Success
Survival Skills for the African-American Woman
Overcoming the SuperWoman Syndrome

Forthcoming Books:
You're on Stage! Image, Etiquette, Branding & Style
Women's Journey to Wellness: Mind, Body & Spirit
A Woman's Survival Guide for Obstacles, Transition & Change
Women a Leaders: Strategies for Empowerment & Communication
Beyond the Body: Developing Inner Beauty
The Young Man's Guide for Personal Success
Emotional Wellness for Women Volume I
Emotional Wellness for Women Volume II
Emotional Wellness for Women Volume III
The Baby Boomer's Handbook for Women

These books will be available from the individual contributors, the publisher (www.prowoman.net), Amazon.com, and your local bookstore.